DON'T SINK---
SWIM TO SUCCESS

Deep Lessons of Life

By Rolland G. (Rollie) Riesberg

(a family autobiography with helpful lessons
for a successful life)

FREE BOOK from

Rollie

This book may be ordered through booksellers or by contacting the Printer, BookLogix®, 1264 Old Alpharetta Rd., Alpharetta, GA 30005
www.booklogix.com
(470) 239-8547

In the preparation of the Financial Section of this book, every effort has been made to offer the most current, correct and clearly expressed information possible. Nonetheless, inadvertent errors can occur and investment rules and regulations often change. Further, the information in the text is intended to afford general guidelines on matters of interest to individual investors. The application and impact of investment rules and laws can vary widely, however, from case to case based upon the specific or unique facts involved. Accordingly, the information in this book is not intended to serve as legal, accounting or investing advice. Readers are encouraged to consult with professional advisors for advice concerning specific matters before making any decision; the author disclaims any responsibility for positions taken by investors in their individual cases or for any misunderstanding on the part of readers of this book.

ACKNOWLEDGEMENTS

(Please refer to SPECIAL SECTION B. "<u>Thank You</u>" for additional
Acknowledgements.)

TABLE OF CONTENTS

SPECIAL SECTION
A. Family Personal Profiles

DON'T SINK--- SWIM TO SUCCESS

Deep Lessons of Life

INTRODUCTION

This book is not about the ocean liner Titanic. It is not about water sports. What this book is about is <u>Survival</u>. Survival from well-meaning (supposedly) but wrong-doing, wrong-thinking, abusive relatives. If friends treated you this way, you could make them ex-friends real quick. But family members who are verbally and emotionally abusive, you are stuck with them------for life!

All my life I have had deep compassion for people who were abused emotionally and verbally, not to mention physically. During my youthful school years, I would come to the defense of those "underdogs" who were being abused by their school-mates. Sometimes me running interference for my friend underdogs would cause me to be put in the same underdog category by the school-mate abusers. Most of my best friends were underdogs. One of the main reasons I am writing this book is to "run interference" for our abused familymembers.

I will not say that I do not know why I am writing this book. I do know why. I am writing this book for five reasons:

(1) To help other people who are in the same boat as our family members (and it is sinking fast). We have 4 couples who are our best friends who are being verbally and emotionally abused by their family members.

(2) To share our testimony of how God has gotten those family members through these most difficult years of their life.

(3) To help others be in position to take advantage of the talent God has given me, my knowledge, education and experience in the realm of Finance, Economics and Money-management.

(4) To provide the truth and our family history for interested family members and our friends and associates.

(5) And most important of all, to leave an indelible legacy showing what Jesus has meant to us and our lives and to be a dedicated witness for Him. Still, I cannot believe I am writing a <u>book</u>. I have a strong background in Technical writing but not for an autobiography. All I can say is that God is "pushing" me to write this book to help others who are "hurting and in need". And the <u>hurting</u> sometimes is so severe and unbearable, that there have been some who have taken their own lives to protect themselves from any further abuse.

Do you want your life to end in failure or do you want it to be a success? If you will <u>swim</u> toward the goal God has set for you and your life and Him, you will achieve ultimate success and you will not sink or fail.

CHAPTER 1.

Sink or Swim---It's Your Choice

Normally each family has at least one or two people who are doling out verbal and emotional abuse on a regular and continual basis to certain other family members. With this, the abused family members have 2 choices----to sink or to swim. To sink, they would be giving in to the abuse and giving up, sinking to the lowest possible depths----which could be fatal to them. Hopefully for them, they will choose to swim (change direction in their lives to move beyond this verbal and emotional abuse).

I will share with you some of the comments that have been made, either verbally or in written form for family problem-solving meetings (I know many of these same comments you will be able to identify with):

- We don't need you for parents anymore (we have my wife's or husband's parents).
- You and Mom are different from my wife's or husband's parents (which makes you bad).
- You and Mom raised me wrong (you were always telling me what to do and were making decisions for me).

- You and Mom need to make a life for yourself and make lots of friends.
- My wife/husband and I don't want to have to consider you anymore when making family decisions.
- We have our own family responsibilities--- we do not have time for you.
- My wife/husband does not like some of the things you say and do and the way you look.
- My wife/husband cannot stand Mom or Dad.
- We do not want to take money from you because it makes us feel like you are trying to control us.
- On the other hand, my husband/wife is upset because you stopped giving us financial assistance.
- My wife/husband and I are too busy and tired to help move Mom and Dad or to help with anything.
- My wife/husband has so many family members (very big family) coming to stay with us all of the time, there is no room or time for <u>my</u> children to come visit and stay with us. My home has become the "Family Hilton Hotel" for my wife's/husband's family---for <u>Free</u>.
- We don't need you for friends, Mom and Dad, we have plenty of friends already.

- Dad/Mom, I know how very sick Mom/Dad is, but I cannot help you with her/him---I have responsibilities for my <u>own</u> family.
- We don't need your help with anything or advice---we want to make our own mistakes and learn from them.
- My husband/wife doesn't want to also be <u>your</u> son/daughter; he/she already has parents.

The emotional abuse is far worse than all of the verbal abuses combined. And the <u>top</u> emotional abuse is the refusing to allow grandparents to see their precious grandchildren, often times for many months at a time or sometimes never. Surely these abusive family members can find a more creative way to <u>torture</u> the grandparents.

In writing this book, my intentions are good. My intentions are to "awaken" the responsible parties as to their actions and to help you, the readers of this book, who may be experiencing similar family problems.

Once the abused family members decide to <u>swim</u> and change the direction in their lives, their lives will change for the better. You cannot change people and their thought processes--- only God can change people. And in some cases, it may even take a miracle to bring them to their senses. We only have control over ourselves and our own thought processes. I know none of us are perfect---we have our own faults. However, the abused family members have respected the abusive family member's <u>reasonable</u> wishes. Upon weighing all of the issues (problems), some of the abused family members decided it best to change direction and move on with their lives--- without the abusive family members being included in their lives---it was their choice. This has not been an easy decision for the abused family members but it has been <u>survival</u> for them. And as part of this, they have tried to identify and dwell on the positives. No matter how bad or mean a person may be, they still have some good in them. Whatever it takes to <u>survive</u> this onslaught of verbal and emotional abuse, they must do it and move on with their lives.

     <u>Survival</u>: What will their <u>new</u> lives be like? Their lives, and yours, could entail the following (whatever works):

        (1) Start a Club with your friends who are in the same boat. The Club could be called the "<u>Abused Family Members Survival Club</u>". Members could meet once a week, for lunch or dinner, to take care of club business and tell "war stories" and share ways to help one another.

        (2) Club members/friends need to "lean on one another" and pray a lot. This

thing is too big for them to handle by themselves---if they will just turn it over to God and let Him carry them through.

(3) Act indifferent toward the "abusers"---- ignore them! Reflecting back to our childhood school days: The extra-sensitive and unusual looking, shaped and sized kids always received a lot of negative and hurtful kidding. Most of the time, this was the way the "kidders" kept themselves amused and entertained. For the most part, adults are nothing but big kids (supposedly grown up). Ignore these abusers who are using the abused for their <u>cheap</u> entertainment---move on!

(4) Get busy and stay busy in your lives doing something worthwhile for others who are also hurting and need help.

(5) Write a book and publish it! Don't laugh---it will <u>really</u> keep you <u>busy</u> and help you to put this, your problem into proper perspective, helping you to move on with your life. Remember, it is <u>your</u> choice to either, Sink or Swim.

CHAPTER 2.

Family Members Abusing Other Family Members

Why are these abusive family members abusing other family members? Maybe the abusive family members have decided they don't like the way the abused look, talk or act. Maybe the abused don't mind well or take orders, Maybe the abusers are "Control Freaks" and want to be in control of everything and everybody.

Of course, physical abuse may also be involved and that presents another set of problems which must be dealt with in different ways---but immediately and effectively!

If you have had the misfortune of having abusive people in your family doling out verbal and emotional abuse, you might ask, "What's wrong with these people? What makes them act this way?" For one thing, they may all have strong, controlling personalities; many people refer to them as "Control Freaks" ---I have a tendency to use the latter description.

When someone is perpetually acting abnormal in their lives, I try to analyze them to try to find out why they act that way. Let's take a look at some of the reasons/backgrounds that could cause a family member become a "Control Freak":

(1) Maybe that person had parents who were extremely permissive and did not know how to raise or what to do with children in the first place.

(2) Maybe the child (toddler) was so strong-willed that the parents gave in early on, letting the child make all of his or her own decisions about <u>everything</u>.

(3) Maybe the child was dropped on its head (only kidding).

(4) Maybe that person was born with a chemical imbalance in the brain (I'm being nice).

(5) Maybe it's a generational thing where the women in the family are born into "Queendom" and are raised up to be Queens and the fathers and sons are relegated to life-long serfdom and obedience (for difficult males, there is an Obedience School to straighten them out).

(6)   Maybe that person is so afraid of losing control, they have to maintain <u>constant</u> control of those around them.

(7)   Maybe that person is <u>so</u> riddled with inferiority complexes, he or she has to always "keep the upper hand".

(8)   Maybe that person's parents never reprimanded the child or told them "no".

(9)   Maybe the child's parents outright spoiled the child to the point where the child was <u>so</u> egocentric that no one could stand to be around that person.

(10) Maybe that person had so many brothers and sisters (like 18 to 20 of them), and as the oldest sibling, was put in charge by the parents of helping to raise all of the younger children.

(11) Maybe that person has developed the mindset that anything or anyone that is <u>different</u> from what he or she was exposed to as a child represents a "threat" to security and normal well-being.

(12) Maybe that person is <u>so</u> riddled with fears of all kinds he or she is afraid to make friends, be a friend, or to "become vulnerable" to anyone or anything that has a connection with people.

Some or our abused family members are being verbally and emotionally abused by their grown, adult children and their spouses because the parents are trying to offer advice and help them have a better life than what they had. The parents have no choice but to <u>release</u> and set the abusive children free. I know the parents love their son or daughter and will always love them and be concerned about their well-being, no matter what they say or do. But the parents have to "turn loose" and start a <u>new</u> life for themselves, even if it means them telling the abusive adult children, "I don't care anymore what you do in the future---it is your life."

<u>Family Relationships</u>: Fortunately, there are families where family ties and love is strong. This is even the case between a family and the in-law's family. But, the number of families with "Control Freaks" seems to be growing. In "times of need", your family is always supposed to "be there for you"---but that is not necessarily so anymore. Sometimes, your best friends and Church member friends are better to you than your own close, immediate family members.

CHAPTER 3.

Hard Times and Good Times (and Opportunities)

It is often said that "hard times builds character". Well, all I can say to that is, "there must be a lot of characters running around out there." God never promised that life would be easy. Yes, easy, good times are very easy to take. We didn't know it at the time, but some of the best times in our lives were when we were dating our spouse-to-be, when we got married (if we married Mr. or Mrs. <u>Right</u>, respectively) and when our children were born and in their younger years. Also, for the children who grew up loving and respecting their parents. But for those children who grew up to develop a keen sense for the art of verbal and emotional abuse with a general distaste for their parents, the abused parents must learn to develop ways to deal with them and move on. If channeled properly, abused parents can use that adversity in their life to build strength on for your <u>new</u> life with God guiding them.

I will now share with you the Hard Times in my life I used to draw strength from to develop determination for the later years of my life. My wife calls that determination "stubbornness" but I like to think of it as <u>creative determination</u>.

Without any hesitation, one of the hardest times of my life was when I was 4 years old and my Mom and Dad divorced. I carried that "guilt" with me until I became an adult. I remember standing between my Mom and Dad in some motel room somewhere between San Diego, CA and Pawhuska, OK with my Dad looking down at me and asking, "Rollie, do you want to stay with me, or do you want to go see your Grandmother, Nan?" Of course, since I hadn't seen my Grandmother in a long time, I picked going to see Nan. The next thing I remembered was my Dad stopping the car, letting my Mom and I out at Nan's house and driving away. Most children don't even remember things that happened to them when they were 3 or 4---but I did. (I carried that burden of guilt with me all of my childhood years, blaming myself for my Mom and Dad getting a divorce.)

Then there were the "going hungry" years. About a year later, when I was 5, I remember being so very hungry and going to my Mom, crying and telling her that "my tummy hurts". I remember her telling me to drink lots of water. She gave me a few of the remaining crackers from a Saltine Cracker box, the only thing left to eat in the house. She told me, "if we could make it for 4 or 5 days, the check would come in and then we would have money to buy lots of food." I don't know if the check was an allotment check from my Step-father who was in the Army at Fort Sill, OK and if they had gotten married by then or not. (My Mom and I had moved out on our own away from Nan and Gramps, my grandparents.) Anyway, those indelible memories of being so hungry caused me to start working at the age of 7 selling Cloverine Brand salve, American Seed Company garden & flower seeds, Cardinal and Gibson greeting cards, and a year later, mowing lawns using a "push" reel-type mower---to have money in my pocket so that when my brothers (half) and I got hungry, I could go buy something for us to eat.

Don't misunderstand me, when World War II was over and my Mom and Step-father had already gotten married, we had plenty of money and lots of good food for about 2 ½ years (my Step-father had a good job as a Carpenter making good money).

Then, one day at work, the ladder fell with my Step-father on it. His right arm was "crushed" at the elbow, and in healing, set-up stiff. From then on, he relied on gambling (cards, dominoes, billiards and betting) to make a living for the family. For the most part, he lost a lot more money than he won. Often times, he would be gone from home for 2, 3, 4 weeks or longer, at a time (we didn't know where he was). I would ride my bicycle all over town (small town of Pawhuska, population of 5000 people) trying to find him and sometimes I couldn't. If I found him and he was winning, he would give me 2 or 3 dollars so I could go buy some food for the family (back then, the price of bread was 19 c a loaf and hamburger meat was 29 c a pound). If I found him and he was losing, he would say, "sorry Son, I don't have any money---I am losing." One thing that puzzled me all of those years---my brothers, Mom and I didn't have any money for food---but somehow, my Mom and Step-father always had money to buy cigarettes, and as time went on, also for beer.

Since things weren't working out very well for the family, my Mom decided that we needed to move to Tulsa to start a new life. There were numerous reasons to make the change of scenery: 1) I had just finished the 7th grade of Junior High school and had a good friend in the neighborhood who was always getting into trouble and was a bad influence on me. 2) My Step-father was getting into trouble in many ways. 3) To sell our house and pay-off as many of our debts as we could (we owed money to almost every business in town---grocery store charge accounts were "maxed out"). 4) To find real job opportunities for my Step-father that a large city has to offer and 5) To have better schools for my brothers and me.

Once we moved to Tulsa, with the new environment, the quality of our lives gradually started improving. And for 2 years, things were going well. For one thing, we had food again---plenty of it (and Mom was a good cook---she learned from my Grandmother, Nan, who was the VERY BEST). My Step-father enrolled in Aircraft Welding at Spartan School of Aeronautics and got a real job as a commercial delivery milkman for Carnation Dairies.

Then, all of a sudden, things started "falling apart". (My Step-father quit Welding school and lost his job at Carnation.) What happened next? He started reverting to his "old ways". But this time, the physical violence between him and Mom resumed and got a lot worse. By this time, Mom started drinking, along with some "running around". Fortunately, I wasn't home much---I was quite busy going to high school and working part time 6 days a week (one night off) as a Cashier/Stocker at a major super market (Standard Humpty Dumpty)---being close to <u>food</u> again!

Then, finally, after graduating from high school, I got my chance to <u>escape</u>---I joined the U.S. Air Force for 4 years and was assigned a job as a B-47 Jet Aircraft Mechanic. And the food (from the Chow Hall) was <u>great</u>! But---I hated leaving my Brothers behind (they had it worse, far worse, than I did when I was living at home)!

The second hardest time of my life was when my Dad died on July 28, 1978 of a sudden heart attack. My Wife and I, our Son and my Wife's parents were on vacation in the Hawaiian Islands. We were staying at a hotel in Kauai the night before we were to fly to Honolulu the next morning for a week's visit with my Dad and Step-mother who lived in Kaneohe. (That evening, we got a telephone call from the Pastor of my Dad and Step-mother's church telling us that my Dad had passed away that day.) I was <u>devastated</u>---words cannot describe how very much I was hurting on the inside! We caught the first flight to Honolulu early the next morning. My Step-mother and Step-sister met us at the airport. The first words out of my Step-mother's mouth were: "You've killed your father! Why didn't you call him? He was worried sick over you!" You can imagine how I felt! I wanted to die and join my Dad!

My Step-mother was evading the truth: A couple of days before we left home to fly to Hawaii for our week-long vacation to the islands of Maui and Kauai and then to Honolulu to spend another week with Dad and Julie (my step-mother), we sent Dad and Julie a letter giving them our schedule and itinerary. (I also called them from California when we were changing flights.) My Wife's mom and dad (at my Dad's invitation) were going to stay with Dad and Julie for 2 more weeks after Loretta, Doug and I left to return home to Atlanta. This was my Dad's idea when he came to visit us and Loretta's parents for the Christmas holidays 7 months before he died. (This was the first time my Dad came to visit us without bringing my Step-mother; she opted to go to Guam to visit her family for Christmas instead.) Anyway, Loretta's parents had never been to Hawaii and my Dad thought it would be a great treat for them to come to Hawaii with us and stay for 2 extra weeks so that he and Julie could give them the "Royal Treatment". I purposely did not call Dad and Julie once we arrived in Maui---I did not want them to fly to Maui to join us because my Step-mother, for the "Control Freak" she was, would have ruined Loretta's parents' Hawaiian vacation. (My Step-mother, a few days after my Dad died, informed me that she and Dad were planning on doing that very thing---joining us for our vacation in Maui and Kauai.) I couldn't bring myself to tell Julie the real reason why I didn't call from Maui, because it would have hurt her.

It took me over a year to get out of the "I don't want to live" mental mode---and my Step-mother's statement to me, "you've killed your father" didn't help. Had it not been for my wonderful, loving Wife and Son's support, I probably would have died and joined my Dad in Heaven (I knew Loretta and Doug needed me).

Three days after my Dad died, Loretta and I went to visit my Dad's best friend, Kenneth Arakaki, who lived in the house immediately behind Dad's house. Kenneth was so very kind to tell Loretta and I what really caused my Dad's death: All that morning, the day before we were to fly to

Honolulu to visit my Dad and Step-mother at their home in Kaneohe, Dad and Julie were arguing intensely over the statement she made to Dad, "that we nor Loretta's parents could stay with them as Dad had planned" because some of <u>her</u> relatives were coming to visit and <u>they</u> were going to stay with them instead. My Step-mother "stormed out of he house", drove off and was gone until early evening. My Dad was "drinking heavily" and spent most of the late morning and most of the afternoon visiting with Kenneth who said that he told my Dad repeatedly, "that he was drinking too much and that he ought to quit". (My Dad was taking Blood Pressure medicine and should not have been drinking much.) Anyway, after drinking heavily most of the day, my Dad walked home to get some more beer from the Refrigerator---my Dad was found lying on the floor in front of the Refrigerator, dead from a massive heart attack. (My Step-mother dealt with her own guilt by shifting it to <u>me</u>!)

To make matters worse, my Dad died without a Will and all assets/property were held in Joint Tenancy with Right of Survivorship. The next business day after my Dad died, I noticed that my Step-mother and Step-sister were very busy "taking care of business". I discovered later on that what they were doing was moving most of the assets and real estate property into the Trust my Step-mother's first husband (last name Arnold) left for her when he died in his late 30s. I was hurt even more since my Dad didn't remember me, his <u>only</u> child, or our Son, his <u>only</u> grandson in any way. I asked my Step-mother to give me Dad's Daily Concordance Bible which he read to me and shared with me several times when he visited with us that last December before he died; I also asked for his Guitar and Wristwatch---my Step-mother refused! Years later, a few years before my Step-mother died, I asked her again for Dad's Bible and Guitar---she responded, "the termites ate them". After my Step-mother died, my Step-sister ended up with all of the assets/property via the Trust. (She eventually sent me some of my Dad's personal belongings from his work, e.g. his desk name plate, photos (family and work), awards, and a Bible given to him as an award, etc.) I am grateful for that kind gesture on the part of my Step-sister. <u>A word of advice</u>: Do not take love and affection for granted. <u>Show</u> your love, <u>tell</u>

your love on a regular basis---"actions speak louder than words" but also, show the person you care about them! If you love someone, at least leave them some personal item like your wristwatch, senior ring or something to let them know you cared about them while you were alive. <u>DO NOT</u> take anything for granted!

The next hardest time for me and my brother, Jimmy (Brian, as he now prefers) was when we lost our "baby brother" Winky (Bill, as he preferred) to Cancer of the Stomach (Peritoneal Wall) in September of 2006. For the first few months after Winky's death, Jimmy and I had extreme difficulty accepting the loss. But gradually, we began to see that God brought Winky home to be with Him to <u>end</u> his relentless, excruciating pain, nausea and suffering.

More recently, my Wife, Loretta, in April of 2008, had Colon/Rectal Cancer Surgery. Her recovery, at the time, progressed fairly well thanks to God's love and care and the exceptional care from her doctors, nurses, and hospital and therapy staff members. (We had put our total faith and trust in God that He would ultimately heal Loretta.)

Now, so much for the Hard or Bad Times! I want to elaborate on the <u>Good Times</u> in my life which are so much more pleasant and memorable.

-<u>My Grandmother, Nan's Cooking</u>: I know I am being prejudicial but she was literally the "best cook in the whole wide world"! While we lived in Pawhuska, OK, many times she kept my brothers and me from going hungry---and with such delight! As a matter of fact, in the earlier years, when my Mom and my Uncle George were young children (around the ages of 5 and 3), Nan was hired by the Governor of Oklahoma to be <u>the</u> Cook for the family and the Nanny for he and his wife's children. Of course, Nan had no choice but to put her children, Mae and George, in a Catholic Orphanage nearby since whey were not allowed to live with her in the Governor's Mansion.

-<u>Birthday and Christmas Gifts from My Dad</u>: My Mom and Dad were divorced and my Dad lived far away in Hawaii. Most of the time, the gifts were in the form of $25 or $50 checks, and a couple of times $100 checks. When I would get $50 or $100 gifts, I would think, Dad <u>really</u> loves me and is proud of me. Then, there were a couple of times when I received nothing---no card, not anything. (Then I would think, Dad doesn't love me; he is mad at me; I've done something wrong.) As you can see, I literally worshiped my Dad---he was my

God, my Jesus until I got grown and met the Real Jesus, thanks to my Wife and Sunday school teacher.

-When I Was With My Dad: I did not get to be with my Dad very often, since I lived with my Mom in Oklahoma and he lived in Hawaii. I distinctly remember those wonderful times---in 1942, 1945, 1948, 1953 (summer, 2 months, 2 days in Hawaii), 1956 (my high school graduation and 4 weeks driving trip to visit Riesberg relatives in Colorado, Minnesota and Wisconsin), 1959 (on 28 day vacation leave in Hawaii while in the U.S. Air Force). After Loretta and I married, we got to see my Dad more frequently (thanks to Delta Air Lines free travel and reduced-rate passes on other air lines).

-My Mom Frequently Telling Me She Loved Me and Was Proud of Me: My Mom often told me that some day when I am grown, I would be a Governor or a Concert Pianist or some other famous person. For the 2 good years, while we were living in Pawhuska, with my Step-father having a good-paying Carpenter job, my Mom and Step-father ("Pop" as I called him) bought me a nice, used Baby Grand piano and paid for my lessons. But, after that, my talent began to wane and the extra money quickly vanished since Pop lost his job because of an injury. (I really do appreciate the opportunity they gave me with the piano lessons and the piano!) My Step-father was as good to me as he was to his own sons (my 2 half-brothers). He called me "son" just like he called them "son" and he never spanked me or raised his voice to me. My brothers weren't so lucky!

-The 5 Years (1948-52) I Had Fireworks Stands: That year, 1948 was the year my Step-father fell off of a ladder and crushed his right arm at the elbow. The money "dried up" quickly and we started going hungry. And there I was, always trying to find ways to make money. I had broken the "bad news" to my Piano Teacher, Mrs. Elaine Poe, that we no longer had money and I was going to have to stop my lessons. I told her that I was looking for a job. She reminded me that her husband, Marcus Poe had a Wholesale Distributorship business. She asked if I would like for him to set me up with a Fireworks Stand selling fireworks. I told her that I loved fireworks, and since it was about 4 weeks before July 4th, my reply was, "yes, yes, yes!" I liked it so much, I had Fireworks Stands for 4 more years after that year (3 in Pawhuska while we lived there; 2 in Pawhuska after we moved to

Tulsa). Those 2 years I rode the Continental Trail-Ways Bus back to Pawhuska and stayed with my Grandparents. I missed them so very much and this gave me an opportunity to be with them again---and to eat Nan's DELICIOUS cooking again!

 -Having 2 Brothers to Love and Care For: God gave me my 2 Brothers to teach me, early in my life, how to truly love and care for someone else other than myself. Words cannot describe how much joy I received from taking care of my "little brothers". I started working for money when I was 7 years old (then I had money in my pocket to buy food for the 3 of us when we were hungry). My Brother's Birthdays and Christmas' were really special for me.

 -The Day I Met My Wife-To-Be (The Love of My Life): There she sat, there in the Shreveport, LA Operations office of Delta Air Lines, waiting for the aircraft she had been working to come back from Houston, TX so she could get back on the aircraft and work the flight back to Memphis, TN, her Home Base. (She had to be taken off the flight at Shreveport for being sick--- throwing up and everything that goes with air sickness.) Can you imagine---a stewardess getting air sick every time the aircraft took off!! Anyway, I came to work early and there she sat, the cutest, prettiest redhead I had ever seen in my whole life! I asked her (jokingly), "What are you doing here? You are supposed to be out there working a flight!" She replied with a cute smile, "I got sick." I introduced myself and said, "I have some spare time before I start to work. Let me take you into Dobbs House (Terminal Restaurant) and buy you a piece of apple pie and a glass of milk---it will make you feel a <u>lot better</u>." (And it did!) When her flight came back to Shreveport, she got on and worked it back to Memphis----and she did not get sick this time. Her name was Laurie Robertson and we started out being real good friends. She was so caring and so easy to talk with. We dated for 3 years before we got married---but I believe I started loving her that moment I first saw her!

-<u>The Day We Had Our One and Only Child, Our Son</u>: We waited all day long for Rolland <u>Douglas</u> Riesberg to be born. Laurie's (now Loretta) mother, Marietta took her to the hospital there in Memphis at 6:30 that morning when Loretta's "water broke". I flew in from Atlanta that morning at 9:00. At 8:55 that evening, little Doug finally arrived! (Of course, he was the prettiest boy-baby we had ever seen!) I was so proud of him! Now I had someone to be "<u>best pals</u>" with---a father and son relationship that I always wanted my Dad and I to have but couldn't because of the more than 3000 miles (Oklahoma to Hawaii) that always separated us. Loretta and I have always loved our Son, Doug so very much and we are very proud of him!

CHAPTER 4.

Be Kind to Others----Stress Can Kill

Be kinder than necessary, for everyone you meet is fighting some kind of battle. Live simply, Love generously, Care deeply----Leave the rest to God.

There is no definitive reason why we should say and do hurtful things to people. We may not know it but the person we are being verbally and emotionally abusive to may secretly love and admire us. Like I always say jokingly, "Be kind to everyone because you never know who is going to be your Boss some day."

Yes, stress can kill a person. Research shows that a weakened immune system can lead to cancer. A strong immune system seeks out and destroys cancer cells. Cancer cells are prevalent in everyone's body but a strongly healthy immune system will keep cancer cells in the body subdued.

In my search efforts to help the readers of this, my book has produced the following research results as compiled by the **National Cancer Institute:**

National Cancer Institute at the National Institutes of Health

Fact Sheet **(Revised: 12/10/2012)**

Psychological Stress and Cancer

Key Points:

-Psychological stress alone has not been found to cause cancer, but psychological stress that lasts a long time may affect a person's overall health and ability to cope with cancer.

-People who are better able to cope with stress have a better quality of life while they are being treated for cancer, but they do not necessarily live longer.

1. What is psychological stress?

Psychological stress describes what people feel when they are under mental, physical, or emotional pressure. Although it is normal to experience some psychological stress from time to time, people who experience high levels of psychological stress or who experience it repeatedly over a long period of time may develop health problems (mental and/or physical).

Stress can be caused both by daily responsibilities and routine events, as well as by more unusual events, such as a trauma or illness in oneself or a close family member. When people feel that they are unable to manage or control changes caused by cancer or normal life activities, they are in distress. Distress has become increasingly recognized as a factor that can reduce the quality of life of cancer patients. There is even some evidence that extreme distress is associated with poorer clinical outcomes. Clinical guidelines are available to help doctors and nurses assess levels of distress and help patients manage it.

The fact sheet provides a general introduction to the stress that people may experience as they cope with cancer. More detailed information about specific psychological conditions related to stress can be found in the Related Resources and Selected References at the end of this fact sheet.

2. How does the body respond during stress?

The body responds to physical, mental, or emotional pressure by releasing stress hormones (such as epinephrine and norepinephrine) that increase blood pressure, speed heart rate, and raise blood sugar levels. These changes help a person act with greater strength and speed to escape a perceived threat.

Research has shown that people who experience intense and long-term (i.e. chronic) stress can have digestive problems, fertility problems, urinary problems, and a weakened immune system. People who experience chronic stress are also more prone to viral infections such as the flu or common cold and to have headaches, sleep trouble, depression, and anxiety.

3. Can psychological stress cause cancer?

Although stress can cause a number of physical health problems, the evidence that it can cause cancer is weak. Some studies have indicated a link between various psychological factors and an increased risk of developing cancer, but others have not.

Apparent links between psychological stress and cancer could arise in several ways. For example, people under stress may develop certain behaviors, such as smoking, overeating, or drinking alcohol, which increase a person's risk for cancer. Or someone who has a relative with cancer may have a higher risk for cancer because of a shared inherited risk factor, not because of the stress induced by the family member's diagnosis.

4. How does psychological stress affect people who have cancer?

People who have cancer may find the physical, emotional, and social effects of the disease to be stressful. Those who attempt to manage their stress with risky behaviors such as smoking or drinking alcohol or who become more sedentary may have a poorer quality of life after cancer treatment. In contrast, people who are able to use effective coping strategies to deal with stress, such as relaxation and stress management techniques, have been shown to have lower levels of depression, anxiety, and symptoms related to the cancer and its treatment. However, there is no evidence that successful management of psychological stress improves cancer survival.

Evidence from experimental studies does suggest that psychological stress can affect a tumor's ability to grow and spread. For example, some studies have shown that when mice bearing human tumors were kept confined or isolated from other mice — conditions that increase stress — their tumors were more likely to grow and spread (metastasize). In one set of experiments, tumors transplanted into the mammary fat pads of mice had much higher rates of spread to the lungs and lymph nodes if the mice were chronically stressed than if the mice were not stressed. Studies in mice and in human cancer cells grown in the laboratory have found that the stress hormone norepinephrine, part of the body's fight-or-flight response system, may promote angio-genesis and metastasis.

In another study, women with triple-negative breast cancer who had been treated with neoadjuvant chemotherapy were asked about their use of beta blockers, which are medications that interfere with certain stress hormones, before and during chemotherapy. Women who reported using beta blockers had a better chance of surviving their cancer treatment without a relapse than women who did not report beta blocker use. There was no difference between the groups, however, in terms of overall survival.

Although there is still no strong evidence that stress directly affects cancer outcomes, some data do suggest that patients can develop a sense of helplessness or hopelessness when stress becomes overwhelming. This response is associated with higher rates of death, although the mechanism for this outcome is unclear. It may be that people who feel helpless or hopeless do not seek treatment when they become ill, give up prematurely on or fail to adhere to potentially helpful therapy, engage in risky behaviors such as drug use, or do not maintain a healthy lifestyle, resulting in premature death.

5. How can people who have cancer learn to cope with psychological stress?

Emotional and social support can help patients learn to cope with psychological stress. Such support can reduce levels of depression, anxiety, and disease-and treatment-related symptoms among patients. Approaches can include the following:

• Training in relaxation, meditation, or stress management
• Counseling or talk therapy
• Cancer education sessions
• Social support in a group setting
• Medications for depression or anxiety
• Exercise

More information about how cancer patients can cope with stress can be found in the PDQ® summaries listed in the Related Resources section at the end of this fact sheet.

Some expert organizations recommend that all cancer patients be screened for distress early in the course of treatment. A number also recommend re-screening at critical points along the course of care. Health care providers can use a variety of screening tools, such as a distress scale or questionnaire, to gauge whether cancer patients need help managing their emotions or with other practical concerns. Patients who show moderate to severe distress are typically referred to appropriate resources, such as a clinical health psychologist, social worker, chaplain, or psychiatrist.

Selected References

1. Atherholt SB, Fann JR. Psychosocial care in Cancer. *Current Psychiatry Reports* 2012;14(1): 23-29. [PubMed Abstract]
2. Fashoyin-Aje LA, Martinez KA, Dy SM. New Patient-centered care standards from the Commission on Cancer; opportunities and challenges. *Journal of Supportive Oncology* 2012; e-pub ahead of print March 20, 2012. [PubMed Abstract]
3. Lutgendorf SK, DeGeest K. Dahmoush L, et al. Social isolation is associated with elevated tumor norepinephtine in ovarian carcinoma patients. *Brain, Behavior, and Immunity* 2011;25(2): 250-255. [PubMed Abstract]

4. Lutgendorf SK, Sood AK, Anderson B, et al. Social support, psychological distress, and natural killer cell activity in ovarian cancer. *Journal of Clinical Oncology* 2005:23(28):7105-7113 [PubMed Abstract]

5. Lutgendorf SK, Sood AK, Antoni MH. Host factors and cancer progression: biobehavioral signaling pathways and interventions. *Journal of Clinical Oncology* 2010;28(26):4094-4099. [PubMed Abstract]

6. McDonald PG, Antoni MH, Lutgendorf SK, etal. A biobehavioral perspective of tumor biology. *Discovery Medicine* 2005;5(30):520-526. [PubMed Abstract]

7. Melhem-Bertrandt A, Chavez-Macgreagor M, Lei X, et al. Beta-blocker use is associated with improved relapse-free survival in patients with triple-negative breast cancer. *Journal of Clincal Oncology* 2011;29(19):2645-2652. [PubMed Abstract]

8. Moreno-Smith M, Lutgendorf SK, Sood AK. Impact of stress on cancer metastasis. *Future Oncology* 2010;6(12):1863-1881. [PubMed Abstract]

9. Segerstrom SC, Miller GE. Psychological stress and the human immune system: a meta-analytic study of 30 years of inquiry. *Psychological Bulletin* 2004;130(4):601-630. [PubMed Abstract]

10. Sloan EK, Priceman SJ, Cox BF, et al. The sympathetic nervous system induces a metastatic switch in primary breast cancer. *Cancer Research* 2010;70(18):7042-7052. [PubMed Abstract]

CHAPTER 5.
Using Your God-given Talents to Help Others

Each one of us has God-given talents which are unique. Even though we were all created equal in God's eyes, each one of us is different---no two people are exactly alike. And with that, each one of us was born with different capacities for learning and different talents. God expects us to learn and develop those talents as much as we can to first, help ourselves and then, to help others. If you are <u>not</u> able to help yourself, you certainly cannot help anyone else!

God expects us to love and care about ourselves---but let's not overdo it to the point of being egocentric and selfish! At the same time, God expects us to love and care about others, as we do ourselves. My Mom, once she started caring as much for others as she did for herself, with God's help, she turned her life around.

As part of caring for ourselves and others, God has provided for us to improve ourselves in all facets of our lives, physically, mentally, emotionally and spiritually. He has also given us opportunities in our lives---<u>opportunities</u> for self-improvement and advancement for the career development portion of our lives. Delta Air Lines gave me the opportunity to work as a Ramp Service Agent on the night shift so that I could attend college during the day. Once I received my B.S. Degree from Memphis State University, I was able to transfer into the Engineering Department at Delta as a Materials & Process Engineer. God expects us to seize opportunities He opens up to us that are within His will. We must have the faith and trust that He will lead us through our lives as He intends. Looking back on my life, Jesus has led me <u>all the way</u>, helping me make the right turns instead of the wrong turns in the "journey of my life". Love Jesus with all of your heart and continually ask Him for guidance and He will always be there for you!

CHAPTER 6
Four Ways of Growth: Physical & Mental, Spiritual and Financial

Physical & Mental Growth

For most of us, God has blessed us with good physical and mental health, with the ability to learn and grow up to be normal, productive, well-meaning adults. But for those who were born with physical and mental health impairments, we need to offer our help to assist them in overcoming their handicap. Many of these handicapped people, with God's love and help, and ours, have grown up to be very successful, productive adults in all facets of their life.

Spiritual Growth

In our Spiritual lives, as in our Physical lives, you either grow and get stronger or you recede and get weaker. Either you will have Jesus in your life (and heart) or you won't. Most people are not big risk takers (risk averse). You may be one of those people. Whether you are or not, you cannot afford to live without Him---the RISK is too great! And it is never too late to ask Jesus for help and to turn your life over to Him.

Financial Growth

God does not expect us to be poor. It has been said many times, "Money does not by happiness"---but then, neither does poverty! If you are financially poor, you cannot help yourself---much less someone else.

Get started NOW planning for your Financial future---it is never too late, but the longer you wait, the harder your money (savings and investments) has to work and the more you have to save/invest for a Secure Retirement and your Financial Future.

CHAPTER 7.

Getting Started---CHARTING The Course for Your Financial Future (FINANCIAL GROWTH)

(Refer to Chart 1—Getting Your Financial House in Order)

PART 1—What You Need to Do NOW

Establish Goals (on paper with targeted dollar amounts) and start saving/investing for each of those goals on a monthly basis. The following is a typical list of Goals in order of importance (first on list being most important):

(1) Establish an Emergency Fund
NOTE: This Fund is needed as a source for money to avoid having to charge or get a bank loan to pay for unexpected emergencies such as car breakdown, home roof leaking, job layoff, etc.; also, to accumulate money to pay cash for larger purchases.

(2) Have adequate insurance protection for Health, Disability, Life, Homeowner's, Car and Long Term Care insurance.

(3) Develop a Budget for Living Expenses; and stay on budget.

(4) Establish a Retirement Plan
NOTES:
a) Take full advantage of your employer's 401(k),
403(b) or 457 Plan, as applicable, especially if there is matching by your employer up to a certain percentage of the dollar amount you contribute monthly.

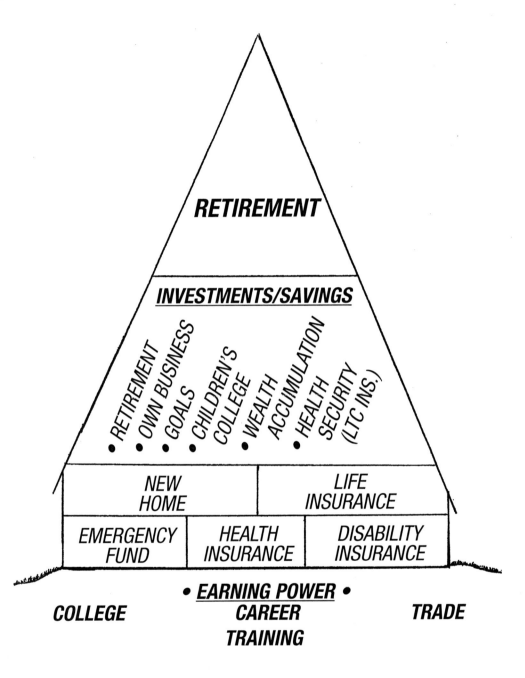

RETIREMENT

INVESTMENTS/SAVINGS

- RETIREMENT
- OWN BUSINESS GOALS
- CHILDREN'S COLLEGE
- WEALTH ACCUMULATION
- HEALTH SECURITY (LTC INS.)

NEW HOME	LIFE INSURANCE	
EMERGENCY FUND	HEALTH INSURANCE	DISABILITY INSURANCE

• **EARNING POWER** •

COLLEGE   **CAREER**   **TRADE**
TRAINING

CHART 1–Getting Your Financial House in Order   by Rollie Riesberg
Financial Growth Services

b) Contribute the maximum yearly to your IRA (Roth or Traditional).

c) If you have a part time business in addition to your full time job, you can also have a Simple IRA, Roth or Single 401(k), or SEP account as long as the IRS maximum allowed annual contribution amount is not exceeded.

(5) Establish an Investment/Savings Plan for future Goals such as: 1) New Home 2) Vacation Home 3) Start a New Business 4) Career Change 5) New Car and 6) Start a Money Fund for higher cost cash purchases.

(6) Establish an Investment/Savings Plan for your Children's College or Trade School expenses.

(Refer to Money Charts 2 & 3 to see how hard Annual and Lump Sum invested money can work for you to help you achieve your monetary goals. These Charts are based on Chart 4 -The Rule of 72 "Compounding Rule".

PART 2—Hard-Workin' Money Hints
(Refer to Chart 5 to see when your Investment/Savings money works the hardest.)

In our modern society, we can obtain money 4 ways:

1) Work for money
2) Let our money work for us
3) Wait around until we inherit money (don't count on it)
4) Accept charity (I don't think so).

PART 3-Ten Rules for Money Managemt.
      (Refer to <u>Chart 6</u> to see how you can <u>best</u>
      manage your money and budget).
These basic rules are guidelines for good,
effective money management, whether it is
for individual families, small businesses or
corporations.

PART 4—What Affects the Stock Market
      (Refer to <u>Chart 7</u> to see the things that
      can have a positive or negative effect
      on the Stock Market and stock prices
      in general.)
In previous years, the main determinants for Stock
Market conditions and levels were the Economy,
Corporate Profits and Interest Rates/Inflation. In
most recent years, Energy Prices and the Threat of
Terrorism have become additional determinants,
making the stock market puzzle more complex and
sometimes more perplexing.

PART 5—Why Wealthy People are Wealthy
      (Refer to <u>Chart 8</u> to find the answers
      to this question.)
It has often been said that many of the Wealthy
people are not necessarily any smarter than most of
the rest of us. But there are distinct reasons why
they have become wealthy:
 1) They work harder.
 2) They take more chances and risks.
 3) They try more things and consequently, have
    more failures, but (this being a "numbers
    game") they also have more successes.

4) They are more in tune with recognizing
   opportunities as they arise.

PART 6—Giving Back (Show His Love------Give)

   (Refer to Chart 9 to see how very blessed we really are and what God expects us to do with our lives.)

God expects us to give: 1) our money 2) our time and 3) our talents helping others who are in need and are not as fortunate as us.

$1,200 per Year at Varying Rates Compounded Annually—End-of-Year Values

Percent	5th Year	10th Year	15th Year	20th Year	25th Year	30th Year	35th Year	40th Year
1%	$ 6,182	$12,680	$ 19,509	$ 26,686	$ 34,231	$ 43,359	$ 50,492	$ 59,250
2	6,369	13,402	21,168	29,739	39,205	49,654	61,192	73,932
3	6,561	14,169	22,988	33,211	45,063	58,803	74,731	93,195
4	6,760	14,983	24,990	37,162	51,974	69,993	91,917	118,592
5	6,962	15,848	27,188	41,662	60,135	83,713	113,803	152,208
6	7,170	16,766	29,607	46,791	69,787	100,562	141,745	196,857
7	7,383	17,740	32,265	52,638	81,211	121,287	177,495	256,332
8	7,603	18,774	35,188	59,307	94,744	146,815	223,322	335,737
9	7,827	19,872	38,403	66,918	110,788	178,290	282,150	441,950
10	8,059	21,037	41,940	75,602	129,818	217,131	357,752	584,222
11	8,295	22,273	45,828	85,518	152,398	265,095	454,996	774,992
12	8,538	23,586	50,103	96,838	179,200	324,351	581,355	1,030,970
13	8,786	24,976	54,806	112,164	211,020	397,578	741,298	1,374,583
14	9,043	26,454	59,976	124,521	248,799	488,084	948,807	1,835,890
15	9,304	28,018	65,660	141,372	293,654	599,948	1,216,015	2,455,144
16	9,572	29,679	71,910	160,609	346,905	726,194	1,560,032	3,286,173
17	9,848	31,440	78,778	182,566	410,115	909,004	2,002,792	4,400,869
18	10,130	33,306	86,326	207,625	485,126	1,119,982	2,572,378	5,895,109
19	10,419	35,284	94,620	236,216	574,117	1,380,464	3,304,696	7,896,595
20	10,716	37,380	103,730	268,831	679,652	1,701,909	4,245,610	10,575,154
21	11,019	39,601	113,736	306,021	804,759	2,098,358	5,453,622	14,156,310
22	11,330	41,954	124,722	348,416	952,998	2,587,006	7,003,256	18,939,087
23	11,649	44,446	136,779	396,727	1,128,558	3,188,884	8,989,333	25,319,371
24	11,976	47,085	150,013	451,758	1,336,360	3,929,683	11,532,334	33,820,458
25	12,310	49,879	164,530	514,417	1,582,186	4,840,641	14,666,342	45,132,982

source: Money Dynamics For The 1980s,
Venita VanCaspel, 1980, Reston Publishing
Company, Inc.

CHART 2 —Annual Money Chart by Rollie Riesberg Financial Growth Services

Securities offered through Great American Advisors®, Inc., Member FINRA
GAA and Financial Growth Services are not affiliated.

Table 1. $10,000 Lump Sum at Varying Rates Compounded Annually—End of Year Values

	5th Yr.	10th Yr.	15th Yr.	20th Yr.	25th Yr.	30th Yr.	35th Yr.	40th Yr.
1%	10,510	11,046	11,609	12,201	12,824	13,478	14,166	14,888
2%	11,040	12,189	13,458	14,859	16,406	18,113	19,998	22,080
3%	11,592	13,439	15,579	18,061	20,937	24,272	28,138	32,620
4%	12,166	14,802	18,009	21,911	26,658	32,433	39,460	48,010
5%	12,762	16,288	20,789	26,532	33,863	43,219	55,160	70,399
6%	13,382	17,908	23,965	32,071	42,918	57,434	76,860	102,857
7%	14,025	19,671	27,590	38,696	54,274	76,122	106,765	149,744
8%	14,693	21,589	31,721	46,609	68,484	100,626	147,853	217,245
9%	15,386	23,673	36,424	56,044	86,230	132,676	204,139	314,094
10%	16,105	25,937	41,772	67,274	108,347	174,494	281,024	452,592
11%	16,850	28,394	47,845	80,623	135,854	228,922	385,748	650,008
12%	17,623	31,058	54,735	96,462	170,000	299,599	527,996	930,509
13%	18,424	33,945	62,542	115,230	212,305	391,158	720,685	1,327,815
14%	19,254	37,072	71,379	137,434	264,619	509,501	981,001	1,888,835
15%	20,113	40,455	81,370	163,665	329,189	662,117	1,331,755	2,678,635
16%	21,003	44,114	92,655	194,607	408,742	858,498	1,803,140	3,787,211
17%	21,924	48,068	105,387	231,055	506,578	1,110,646	2,435,034	5,338,687
18%	22,877	52,338	119,737	273,930	626,686	1,433,706	3,279,972	7,503,783
19%	23,863	56,946	135,895	324,294	773,880	1,846,753	4,407,006	10,516,675
20%	24,883	61,917	154,070	383,375	953,962	2,373,763	5,906,682	14,697,715
21%	25,937	67,274	174,494	452,592	1,173,908	3,044,816	7,897,469	20,484,002
22%	27,027	73,046	197,422	533,576	1,442,101	3,897,578	10,534,018	28,470,377
23%	28,153	79,259	223,139	628,206	1,768,592	4,979,128	14,017,769	39,464,304
24%	29,316	85,944	251,956	738,641	2,165,419	6,348,199	18,610,540	54,559,126
25%	30,517	93,132	284,217	867,361	2,646,698	8,077,935	24,651,903	75,231,638

source: Money Dynamics For The 1980s, Venita VanCaspel, 1980, Reston Publishing Company, Inc.

CHART 3 —Lump Sum Money Chart   by Rollie Riesberg   Financial Growth Services

Securities offered through Great American Advisors®, Inc., Member FINRA   GAA and Financial Growth Services are not affiliated.

The Rule of 72

It's an extremely valuable rule and you'll find it very useful. The Rule of 72 gives you the answer to the question of how long it will take to double your money—to make $1 become $2—at various rates of return.

If you obtain 1 percent on your money, it will take 72 years for $1 to become $2. If you obtain 1.3 percent, it will take 55.4 years; if you obtain 6 percent, it will take 12 years; if you obtain 12 percent. it will take six years; at 18 percent, four years; and at 24 percent it takes three years.

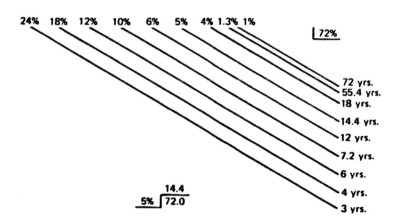

CHART 4 — Compounding Rule   by Rollie Riesberg   source: <u>Money Dynamics For The</u>
   Financial Growth   <u>1980s</u>, Venita VanCaspel, 1980,
   Services   Reston Publishing Company, Inc.

FINANCIAL GROWTH SERVICES
HARD-WORKIN'MONEY HINTS
(What Signs to Watch for-What to Do-When to Do it)

A. **WHEN INTEREST RATES/INFLATION GOES UP!** (Approaching Recession-Bear Market
   1. Stock and bond prices usually go down
   2. Real estate prices usually go down
   3. Gold and other precious metals prices go up
   4. Money market and CD returns go up
   5. Consumer goods prices go up

B. **WHEN INTEREST RATES/INFLATION GOES DOWN!** (Economy Growing-Bull Market)
   1. Stock and bond prices go up
   2. Real estate prices usually go up
   3. Gold and other precious metals prices go down
   4. Money market and CD returns go down
   5. Consumer goods prices go down

C. **ON INTERNATIONAL MONETARY EXCHANGE**
   1. Weak Dollar
      a. Helps U.S. exports
      b. Hurts U.S. imports
      c. Hurts exchange rate

   2. Strong Dollar
      a. Hurts U.S. exports
      b. Helps U.S. imports
      c. Helps exchange rate

D. **COURSES OF ACTION**
   1. If your Debt Interest rate is higher than your savings/Investment Interest Rate-- Pay off your debts.

   2. If your Debt Interest rate is lower than your Savings/Investment Interest rate-- put your money into savings/investments.

   3. Pay cash for everything-- unless you car borrow at a very low interest rate (much lower than the rate your savings/investments will earn).

   4. Mortgage Rates
      a. When Home Mortgage Interest Rates, go up-
         It is a Buyer's Market (Home prices go down)
      b. When Home Mortgage Interests Rates, go down-
         It is a Sellers Market (Home prices go up).

CHART 5—Hard-Workin' Money Hints

Page 1 of 2

5. To Save and Defer Income Taxes, take advantage of
   a. IRA's: Roth, Traditional, Simple
   b. SEP IRA's and Keogh's
   c. TSA (Tax Sheltered Accounts) 403(b)
   d. Employer sponsored 401k, Thrift/Savings, Profit Sharing, Stock   Option and other pension plans.

6. Pay the lowest price for all financial products you are how buying and invest the savings Where the money will work the hardest for you.

NOTE: Financial Products include 1)Home Mortgages 2)Credit cards 3) Home Equity Lines of Credit, etc.

CHART 5 – Hard–Workin' Money Hints (Cont.)   Page 2 of 2

by Rollie Riesberg – Financial Growth Services

Ten rules for money management

1. Plan for the future, major purchases and periodic expenses.

2. Set financial goals. Determine short; mid and long-range financial goals.

3. Know your financial situation. Determine monthly living expenses, periodic expenses and monthly debt payments. Compare outgo to monthly net income. Be aware of your total indebtedness.

4. Develop a realistic budget. Follow your budget as closely as possible. Evaluate your budget. Compare actual expenses with planned expenses.

5. Don't allow expenses to exceed income. Avoid paying only the minimum on your charge cards. Don't charge more every month than you are repaying to your creditors.

6. Save for periodic expenses, such as car and home maintenance. Save five to 10 percent of your net income. Accumulate three to six months' salary in an emergency fund.

7. Pay your own bills on time. Maintain a good credit rating. If you are unable to pay your bills as agreed, contact your creditors and explain your situation. Contact Consumer Credit Counseling Service for professional advice.

8. Distinguish the difference between wants and needs. Take care of your needs first. Money should be spent for wants only after needs have been met.

9. Use credit wisely. Use credit for safety, convenience and planned purchases. Determine the total you can comfortably afford to purchase on credit. Don't allow your credit payments to exceed 20 percent of your net income. Avoid borrowing from one creditor to pay another.

10. Keep a record of daily expenses. Be aware of where your money is going. Use a spending diary to assist you in identifying areas where adjustments need to be made.

CHART 6—Ten Rules for Money Management

by Rollie Riesberg – Financial Growth Services

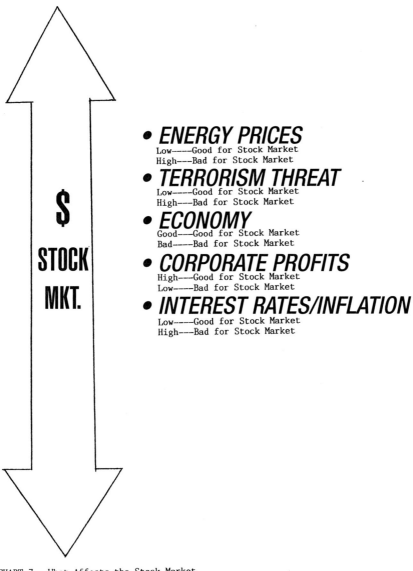

- **ENERGY PRICES**
  Low-----Good for Stock Market
  High---Bad for Stock Market
- **TERRORISM THREAT**
  Low-----Good for Stock Market
  High---Bad for Stock Market
- **ECONOMY**
  Good----Good for Stock Market
  Bad-----Bad for Stock Market
- **CORPORATE PROFITS**
  High---Good for Stock Market
  Low-----Bad for Stock Market
- **INTEREST RATES/INFLATION**
  Low-----Good for Stock Market
  High---Bad for Stock Market

CHART 7——What Affects the Stock Market

by Rollie Riesberg - Financial Growth Services

TITLE: Why Wealthy People are Wealthy

Question: Why are wealthy people wealthy?

1.   Maybe they make big salaries, maybe they don't.

2.   They have a lot more money coming in than they have going out.

3.   They budget and plan their expenditures wisely.

4.   They know how money works hardest. They may even eventually have their money working harder than they are working.

5.   They have the right kind and amount of life insurance.

6.   They are knowledgeable of tax laws and take full advantage of tax savings techniques available to them.

7.   They set financial goals and work toward those goals.

8.   They do not procrastinate.

A.   How does money work hardest?

1.   When it is put into "ownership" investments rather than "loanership" investments - the right place versus the wrong place.

a.   Ownership - Stocks, Mutual Funds, Real Estate, Limited Partnerships, etc.
b.   Loanership - Bonds, Savings Accounts, Treasury Bills/ Bonds, C.D.'s, etc.
c.   Ownership/Loanership Rate of Return/Risk Level:

	Ownership	Loanership
Rate of Return:	loss to no upper limit	low
Risk Level:	low to high	none to low
Stays ahead of Inflation/Taxes:	no to no upper limit	no

2.   When you are willing and able to take higher risk.

3.   If you are spending your money for the right things.

4.   When it is used to buy the right kind and amount of life insurance and amounts of other types of insurance.

5.   When income tax savings techniques are fully utilized.

6.   When time is on your side.

7.   When we give God His share of our income first.

CHART 8— Wealth   Page 1 of 2

B. What is the right kind of life insurance?

    1. Term insurance, of course!(in most cases)
Why? Because term insurance is pure protection and nothing else. Other types such as Whole Life are not pure protection; they have a savings feature built into the policy called "cash value" which is surplus premium paid in earlier years of the policy. You do not get this cash value when you die - only the face value or coverage amount of the policy.

    2. Do not combine insurance protection and savings - never! You need to save/invest on your own, for yourself - and not for the benefit of the insurance company. Buy only pure protection(term life) and invest the difference - for yourself.

    3. Wealthy people have minimal to no life insurance - they are "self insured."

C. How can you save money by knowing about and taking advantage of the tax laws?

    1. By sheltering your investment/savings money from income tax until retirement by utilizing the following:

        a. IRA
        b. Keogh
        c. SEP
        d. 401K
        e. Company Pension/Savings Plan
        f. 403B TSA(Tax Sheltered Account)

    2. Interest paid on primary and secondary home loans is tax deductible.

    3. Business expenses through owning your own business are tax deductible.

CHART 8 — Wealth (cont'd)   Page 2 of 2

by Rollie Riesberg - Financial Growth Services

Theme: SHOW HIS LOVE----GIVE

If we died yesterday--God has has already blessed us so much more than we deserve.
He has showered us with His love in so many ways. Life itself is one of His many
blessings.

We cannot begin to show our appreciation for what He has done for us. In some
small way, we can return to Him a portion of what is already His--our money and our
service.

The money--we ask ourselves, where is the money going to come from? There is too
much month left at the end of the money! Perhaps we are not good enough stewards of
the material possessions God has given us, either through our not knowing how to manage
our money or through our extravagance, or maybe we are in a lower income situation.
Somehow, the money has "slipped through our fingers." How can we be better managers
of our money and stop it from slipping through our fingers?

1. By getting what little amount of savings/investment money we have, working
   harder for us.
2. By taking advantage of all of the tax advantages that are available to us.
3. By having the right kind and amount of insurance protection.
4. By having a properly sized emergency fund set aside so we will not have to
   rely on credit card "plastic money" purchases to meet emergency needs.
5. By being more selective on what we buy and when we buy (Do we really need it;
   do we really have to have it now?).
6. By having a budget and staying within those budget limits (Are we living
   within the boundaries of our income?).
7. By making ourselves set aside a certain amount of money each payday for
   savings/investment (without fail) just like we do giving God back a portion
   of the monetary blessings He has made possible for us to have and use (Pay
   God first, then yourself, then let the bill collectors fight over the rest).

One might think, it is not right to put much emphasis on money and material
things. True--money does not buy happiness--but then, neither does poverty. God does
not intend for us to be poor. He wants us to use the blessings He has given us (our
talents, our intelligence, our knowledge and our time) to His and our best advantage
to the glory of His kingdom. We must use our many blessings to help ourselves, our
fellowman and to serve God the way He intended.

Think about it--Pray about it-- DO IT!

CHART 9 — Giving Back

by Rollie Riesberg - Financial Growth Services

CHAPTER 8.

Now You Are Ready To Enjoy Your New Life (You SURVIVED—You Succeeded—You Made It)

Dear Abused Family Members:

You did not sink—you swam—you did not give up!

This is not a Concluding Chapter of your life—it is a Beginning Chapter of your new life. God has answered your prayers. You have started your new life. Your "abusive family members" are now showing you that they care about and love you again----thank God. We know that God has put forgiveness in your hearts. When we ask God to forgive us of our sins and shortcomings, God forgives us. So, why shouldn't we forgive others who have hurt us---God expects that of us. And you should also ask the abusers for forgiveness for you holding hard feelings and resentment toward them.

Thanks to God, your prayers have been answered. Now that you are in your new life, you must make God the Foundation and Capstone of your new life. You are probably a risk averse (low risk taking) person. So why should you go through the remainder of your life taking the HIGH RISK of not having God in your heart and life------the risk is just TOO GREAT! Asking God to come into your heart may seem like the hardest thing to do, but actually-----it is the <u>easiest</u> thing you will <u>ever</u> do! All you have to do is ask Him to forgive you of your sins and come into your heart and life. And remember, Jesus died for our sins: John 3:16 (For God so loved the world that He gave His only begotten Son, for whosoever believeth in Him shall not perish but have everlasting life).

<u>Our Lives' Final Chapters</u>

As for Loretta and I, we are so thankful to our Heavenly Father for the miracles He gave to Loretta during her 4 years , 10 months battle with colon/rectal cancer. The cancer eventually spread to her liver and on February 7 of last year (2013), God decided to bring Loretta back home to Heaven so she wouldn't suffer any more. My heart is broken----but I am so happy that she is in Heaven with God and Jesus and is no longer hurting. As a tribute to her, God and Jesus, I have added 3 new Chapters to this, my book:
- Chapter 9 – Tribute to Loretta
- Chapter 10 – The Best Phase of My Life ----Witnessing for God
- Chapter 11—Tribute to Our Lord and Savior, Jesus Christ.

I wrote these 3 Chapters in completing Loretta's Book for her: ....*God Bless the Moon and God <u>Blessed Me</u>*.

CHAPTER 9.

Tribute to Loretta

1. In Loving Memory

In Loving Memory
Loretta Claire Riesberg
June 12, 1941 to February 7, 2013

Opening Prayer..........................Dr. Jack May

Trumpet Solo............................Jeremiah Riesberg
                                            Grandson

"Turn Your Eyes Upon Jesus".........Tim Vassar
                                            Mark Giles

"Love Lifted Me".......................Tim Vassar
                                            Mark Giles

Message...............................Dr. Jack May

"Now I Belong to Jesus".............Tim Vassar
                                            Mark Giles

Closing Prayer......................... Dr. Jack May

Pallbearers
Doug Riesberg   Bo Layton
Zachary Riesberg   Tabb Layton
Jeremiah Riesberg   Kevin Frank
Scott Layton   Gabe Ragghianti

pening Prayer...Reverend Hugh Kirby

'rumpet Solo..Jeremiah Riesberg,
                                                            Grandson

I Have Seen the Light"..............................Reverend Hugh Kirby
                                                      Joe and Kim Stanley
                                                      Jon Huff

'Turn Your Eyes Upon Jesus"........................Joe and Kim Stanley
                                                      Jon Huff

'Love Lifted Me"......................................Joe and Kim Stanley
                                                      Jon Huff

Message...Reverend Hugh Kirby

'Now I Belong to Jesus".............................Jon Huff

Closing Prayer.......................................Hugh Kirby

Loretta Claire Riesberg
(June 12, 1941 – February 7, 2013)
Loretta C. Riesberg, our wife, mother,
and Grandmother leaves a legacy of
resourcefulness, creativity, love and
devotion to her family and God. She
was born on June 12, 1941 to Marietta
and Douglas Robertson of Memphis,
Tennesssee and passed away on February
7, 2013 surrounded by her family
and friends. Loretta leaves behind
husband, Rollie, son Doug Riesberg
and his wife Amy, grandchildren
Zachary (15), Jeremiah (11),
Nathaniel (8) and Ethan (7).
She also leaves behind two nieces,
Meredith Layton and husband, Scott
of Knoxville, Tennessee and Ericka Frank
and husband, Kevin of St. Louis, Missouri
and two great nephews Bo and Tabb Layton.

The Lord is my shepherd; I shall not
Want. He maketh me to lie down in
green pastures; he leadeth me beside
the still waters. He restoreth my soul;
he leadeth me in the path of righteousness
for His name's sake. Yea, though I
walk through the valley of the shadow
of death, I will fear no evil: for thou
art with me; thy rod and thy staff they
comfort me. Thou prepares a table
before me in the presence of mine enemies:
thou anointest my head with oil; my cup
runneth over. Surely goodness and mercy
shall follow me all the days of my life
and I will dwell in the house of the Lord
forever.

Psalm 23

2. Come to Me for Rest (Feb. 7, 2013)

February 7

COME TO ME FOR REST and refreshment. The journey has been too much for you, and you are bone-weary. Do not be ashamed of your exhaustion. Instead, see it as an opportunity for Me to take charge of your life.

Remember that *I can fit everything into a pattern for good,* including the things you wish were different. Start where you are at this point in time and space, accepting that this is where I intend you to be. You will get through today one step, one moment at a time. Your main responsibility is to remain attentive to Me, letting Me guide you through the many choices along your pathway.

This sounds like an easy assignment, but it is not. Your desire to live in My Presence goes against the grain of "the world, the flesh, and the devil." Much of your weariness results from your constant battle against these opponents. However, you are on the path of My choosing so do not give up! *Hope in Me, for you will again praise Me for the help of My Presence.*

We are assured and know that [God being a prtner in their labor] all things work together and are [fitting into a plan] for good to and for those who love God and are called according to [His] design and purpose. - Romans 8:28 amp

Why ar hyou in despair, O my soul? And why have you become disturbed within me? Hope in God, for I shall yet praise Him, the help of my countenance and my God. _ Psalm 42:11 nasb

3. Loretta's Letters

A. My Letter to Rollie

Rollie, My (Babe)

    I knew I'd met the love of my life when I first met you. You're the love of my life, I'd like to write more but time is growing short. ~~Rem~~ Remember I love you forever and will be waiting for you. Hold on to your faith and hope. We will be together. Cherish our memories and share them with our grandboys.

B. My Letter to Doug

Doug,

    I'm so sorry I didn't write down the many ways you've blessed my life. You're every thing a son could be. Take care of our precious little boys. I wish I had written earlier and about them. I love them in so many ways too numerous to mention.

4. Rollie's Tribute to Loretta

(1) Missing You So............

My Precious Little Doll:

- I miss your beautiful face and your reassuring smile of sunshine and warmth.
- I miss your loving hold-me-tight hugs and your warm and tender kisses.
- I miss your heart beating so close and in rythym with mine. You have the biggest, softest heart in the whole wide world and universe. When we said "I do", I gave you my heart.
- I miss your caring kindness, sweetness and loving nature.
- I miss your love here on earth but I know you now love me with an even greater love----- a heavenly love. You were and are so very easy-to-love.
- I miss your loving friendship. You were always so easy to talk with and understanding.
- You were my best friend. Now you, God and Jesus are my Best Friends. I am eternally grateful to you for introducing me to God and Jesus! Because of that, I will live with you, God and Jesus in heaven forever!
- I will always love you with all my heart and soul! You are my Precious Little Doll!!!

(2) My Letter to Loretta

February 22, 2013

My Dearest Loretta ⸺

Honey, this world will never be the same because you came. God sent you from Heaven and now He has brought you back home. You saved my life — you brought me to Jesus. Because of you, "I Have truly Seen The Light".

My heart is broken---but I am so happy that you are now at home with Jesus and no longer suffering. You have been so sweet, kind, loving, caring and understanding to me, family, friends and others; you deserve the best Jesus and Heaven has to offer.

I will "Never Say Goodbye" to you--- you are my life, hope, happiness and guardian angel. I am eternally grateful to you and Jesus. You and Jesus are the love of my life!

I love you with all of my heart and Soul and I always will!

Rollie

5. Love Worth Finding Ministries

Article taken from Loretta's Letter to them featured in their Ministry Moments
Newsletter, Sept./Oct. 2012

VISIT US AT LWF.ORG

September-October 2012

Volume 19, Number 5

Love Worth Finding Ministries with
Adrian Rogers

MINISTRY
MOMENTS

HEART TO HEART

GEORGIA

Four years ago, I was diagnosed with cancer and have completed many rounds of radiation and chemotherapy. Having been active in church, I now am unable to attend. Sunday services with Adrian Rogers have literally been an act of God. My husband and I cherish each moment of these services. Pastor Rogers makes the lessons of the Bible come to life.

FROM MICAH

I'm 14 years old and have been listening to Love Worth Finding since I was 8. I have been so impacted by Pastor Rogers and his ministry that I now hope to be a pastor like him one day. Thank you so much for persevering in broadcasting his messages. The whole world needs to hear that God loves them, and that love is truly Love Worth Finding!

6. Letters from Friends and Family

A. Letters from Our Best Friends

Subject: Loretta :)

We were blessed to first get acquainted with Loretta and Rollie about 35 years ago. Together, they have brought such joy and laughter into our lives.

It is a rare thing in this world to see a couple filled with adoration for each other, even through trying circumstances. Rollie and Loretta remained, not only committed, but thoroughly enjoyed each other's company!

Loretta was one of the most thoughtful, caring people we have ever had the pleasure of knowing. Regardless of what was going on with her personally, you would ALWAYS get a smile and positive word from her.

She was also an incredibly intelligent person! She could find solutions for the most complex of problems and many leaned on her for that gift. But of ALL of her gifts, we don't think anyone could match Loretta's creative talent! She could turn an ordinary ball of yarn into the most beautiful things! One treasure she made me [Betty] was a crocheted craft bag for my cross-stitch projects. It was the perfect size and I've enjoyed it so much. I will treasure it even more in years to come. Loretta didn't need patterns and directions to create a marvelous work of art. Her mind worked in a creative way that is simply a gift from God. Although she certainly honed her skills over the years, she was born with a gifting that few posses.

Although our lives are less full without Loretta, heaven is certainly rejoicing with her added presence. We look forward with the hope that we have in Jesus to the day we will all be reunited again, worshipping at His feet.

We are so honored to have known and loved her.

Love, Betty and Malley Gay

Letters from Our Best Friends

We are so thankful for your friendship.
Love you & God bless you forever.
betty & malley

Betty and Malley Gay

Letters from Our Best Friends

Memories of my special friend, Loretta

In October 2008 I knocked on your door...and you opened your heart. From that first meeting, we fast became friends. There you stood, beaming the greatest smile, inviting me into your comfort zone of fabric, yarn, and numerous crafts projects strewn about your Montana timeshare cabin. Just my style! What started out as a business meeting turned into a cherished friendship- a friendship that I continue to draw comfort from each and every day.

We both had so much in common: Love of God and family, nature and wildlife, sewing and crafting, travel and continued learning. Though miles generally separated us, I always felt your kinship when I saw God's wonderful creations. In winter I loved surprising you with photos of deer grazing in our yard or snow and crystals shimmering on bushes and trees. Knowing the joy you received from seeing "our mountains" made me never leave home without a camera. When I learned of your illness I learned of your inner strength- always positive and always respectful of God's plan for your life and your death.

Though we no longer chat on Sundays, your spirit lives among those of other friends and family who continue to "hold me up" when I am "down". I hear your voice and your laugh. I feel your warmth and your love. I feel your strength. Until we meet again, friend, you are in my heart. You will always be a part of me.

Joanne Barsi
Seeley Lake, Montana

Joanne and Mike Barsi

Letters from Our Best Friends

God blessed me with a special friend, <u>Loretta Clair Robertson Riesberg</u>. Loretta and I as infants shared a place in the nursery at Speedway Terrace Baptist Church in Memphis, Tennessee. We witnessed each other being baptized by our pastor Mark Harris after we asked Jesus to come into our hearts as our Lord and Savior.

Going to church and school together, spending the nights with each other, having fun at camps and even double dating, Loretta always stayed the same! She loved the Lord and served Him.

She was my good friend even when we didn't see each other for a few years after moving to different States. She always kept in touch with me remaining the same ole Loretta.

Letters from Our Best Friends

Tim, my husband, remembers that smile of Loretta's lighting up the room when she walked in.

I miss my friend Loretta, but I know I'll see her again in heaven with our Savior when He calls me home.

Thank you Father for blessing me with such a friend as Loretta Risberg.

Lorena (Renie) Lawrence

Proverbs 17:17 "A friend loves at all times, ..."

Lorena (Renie) Maxwell Lawrence

Letters from Our Best Friends

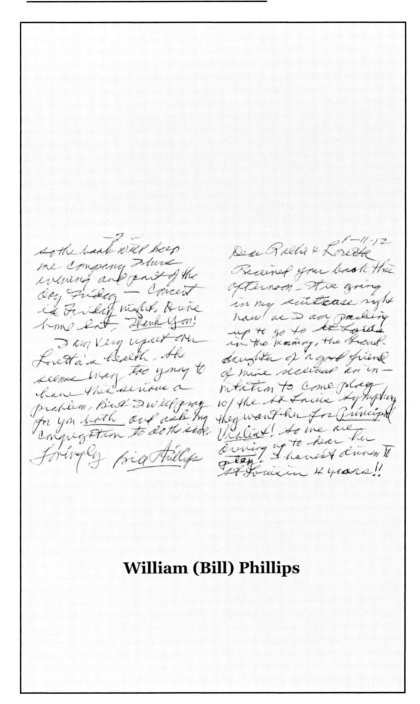

William (Bill) Phillips

Letters from Our Best Friends

Mar. 13, 2013

WILLIAM S. PHILLIPS
500 PRIMROSE COVE
MEMPHIS, TENNESSEE 38117

Dear Rollie

This is a difficult letter for me to write. For one
thing, I am not good with condolensceses. My wife's
passing left me totally alone in Memphis and I do not
function well alone. I have moved to a retirement home
to be around people more, but that has not helped me at
all. I travel a lot, but that seemed to exaserbate the
problem; when I shut the stateroom door, I am alone. The fact
that I was not here for you when you needed me, wanted me to
fulfill Loretta's wish that I play for her funeral, is
very disturbing. So I reached in the desk drawer and
re-read her two letters.

What I got from those two letters was (1) a Woman of faith
and(2) A very strong woman. She had unfailing faith
in her Lord Jesus Christ, and she fought like a tiger to
stay alive for you and her family. I do not know anyone
else who could match that combination as serenly as she
did. I know I couldn't. In April of this year I will
be 88 years old. Thank you God for giving me good health.
Now, I pray for the strngth of Loretta Robertson Riesberg
to carry me through the final years.

Please express my thanks to your son, Douglas, for this thought
thoughtful telephone conversations with me.. And my
sincerest best wishes to you as you complete Loretta's
book for her. And for your continued good health and
well being in the future.

Sincerely.

Bill Phillips

Willism S. Phillips, Ph.D., CPCU., CLU., ARM., CPIA.

A.K.A. "UNCLE BILL." • A.K.A. "WILD BILL" • A.K.A. "WHO ??"

Letters from Our Best Friends

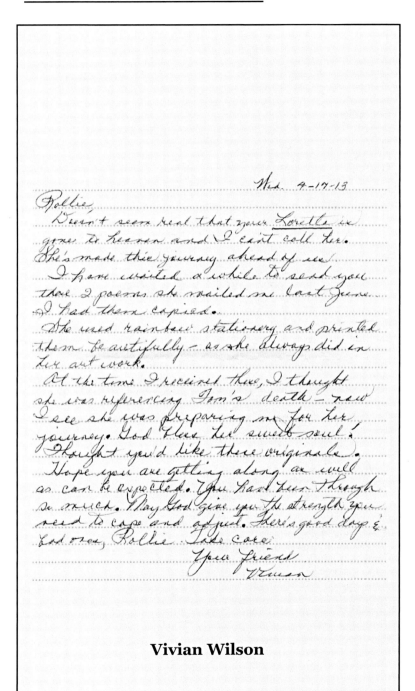

Wed. 4-17-13

Rollie,
Doesn't seem real that your *Loretta* is
gone to heaven and I can't call her.
She's made this journey ahead of us.
I have waited a while to send you
these 2 poems she mailed me last June.
I had them copied.
She used rainbow stationery and printed
them beautifully — as she always did in
her art work.
At the time I received these, I thought
she was referencing Tom's death — now
I see she was preparing me for her
journey. God bless her sweet soul!
Thought you'd like these originals.
Hope you are getting along as well
as can be expected. You have been through
so much. May God give you the strength you
need to cope and adjust. There's good days &
bad ones, Rollie. Take care.
Your friend
Vivian

Vivian Wilson

Jan. 29-68

Dear Rollie & Loretta,

I tried friday night & all day
saturday to call you & even
called the airport, & they said
Rollie was off. So I'm sorry for
I wanted you to know I shared
your happiness. For that was
the day I had wished for you
I would have been there but
I know you both understand
it was hard to tell LeRoy good
bye & keep from crying, as I knew
that would only make him feel
bad. They asked about you Rollie
as they do remember you also
Gaye, Joe never forgotten how
good you are to me. I told
her she would love you
Loretta, as I do. They are moving
to our home town Abilene, Texas

2

untill LeRoy returns from Viet
Nam. Leta, said Walk is expected
to go any day. Rollie are you in
reserve I hope not thats the
first thing that came into my
mind When I head on T. V.
About the reserves being called

Kids, I dont have Walk right
now but I signed up for Luthis
Social Security, & I get $47.00 dollars
a Month state help so you see I
dont have Much but I promise
I'll get you something. you just
Wait + see its pitifull to be poor
but I'm thankfull I am as well
as I am.

Pussy is asleep she is so spoiled
+ so jealous of other cats

Meriah, is fine + says Hello
to you both. We both remembered

3

was on the hour of Ten O'clock the
Morning of the 20th January + how
I Wished I were there,
2 This Will be a short note as
I'm so far behind in my
letter Writing
If you made pictures please dont
Forget Ole Mama Mae I'll never
pay for one are More
Be sweet you two + Write +
tell me all about it
Love + God Bless you both
Always
Mama Mae
Sissy + Miriah

Mama Mae Stroud

Letters from Our Best Friends

-------- Original Message --------
Subject:loretta letter
Date: Sun, 5 May 2013 10:36:55 -0400
From: Mary Lou <lnmmassage@gmail.com>
To:<rgriesberg@bellsouth.net>

Dear Loretta

I most remember Loretta for red hair, easy laugh, and very affirming presence. I loved to see the light shine in her eyes when she spoke of...well, almost everything! Her family, her faith, and even the stories she told on herself when she was a young stewardess with Delta, brought out that light in her. Even when I saw her concerned over something happening with a family member, still she looked for the solution, blessedly assured it was out there somewhere. Such a positive person. I liked to spend time with her, just because anything I was focusing on that wasn't particularly pleasant seemed to fade into something unimportant and trivial. I miss you Loretta. So wonderful to know I will see you again.
Love forever,
Mary Lou
Sunday May 5, 2013

Mary Lou Baer Grover

Letters from Our Best Friends

To my Dear Mrs. Loretta...
for your comfort.

We say	God says	Bible Verses
It's impossible	All things are possible	Luke 18:27
I'm too tired	I will give you rest	Matthew 11:28-30
Nobody really loves me.	I love you	John 3:16 + 3:34
I can't go on	My grace is sufficient	II Corinthians 12:9 Psalms 91:15
I'm not able	I am able	II Cor 9:8
I can't figure things out	I will direct your steps	Proverbs 3:5-6
I can't do it	You can do all things	Philippians 4:13
It's not worth it	It will be worth it	Romans 8:28
I can't forgive myself	I forgive you	1 John 1:9 Romans 8:28

Page 1

Letters from Our Best Friends

We say	God says	Bible Verses
I'm afraid	I have not given you a spirit of fear	II Timothy 1:7
I'm always worried and frustrated	cast all your cares on ME.	I Peter 5:7
I feel alone	I will never leave you or forsake you	Hebrews 13:5
I can't manage	I will supply all your needs	Philippians 4:19
I'm not smart enough	I give you wisdom	I Corinthians 1:30

Jamenia Head
3/7/13

Page 2

Jamenia (Jamie) Head

Letters from Our Best Friends

April, 2012

"You are Loretta!"

Thinking of you in the eve of this day—
Praying for you in every way.
From my heart to yours I sincerely send
Prayers for much strength and your body to mend.

A vivacious, jumping, singing, happy, young girl
So full of zest, her world in a twirl!
That feeling of "Greenlaw" - a world of her own
She felt it, she loved it, it was Loretta's zone!

Stay strong! You're "the Little Engine That Could."
You have that extra "Greenlaw" brave spirit — so
    you'll do what you should.
You're like that engine — you will persevere
until your body responds and healing is here— for
    You Are Loretta!

Hi Loretta & Rollie,
    You know how I love poetry. It's a
wonderful way of saying what is in one's heart & soul
in a different way. I just knew that "You are Loretta!"
Illness is something that is really trying you. But you
are strong in the Lord. I always remember that after
returning from Gloriette you were so empowered — so
filled with His spirit.
    I will continue to pray for you. Stay positive &
strong. "Prayers sent up.
    Blessings come down.
    There's a miracle in the making!"
                            Love You Much,
                            Elizabeth Ann

Elizabeth Ann Gullatt Perry

Letters from Our Best Friends

Laret —

November 24, 2012

I wish that I could be there with you - I would hug you and be near you. But I am near to you in heart, soul, + love. You Know I would give you a "Greenlaw Hug" the Kind you gave all the Kids when we were young.

My son, Paul, said on Thanks-giving, "Mom, God never takes his eyes off us." A car HAD almost hit us + I said "God be with us." Paul said it right you Know.

God put the Robertsons in my life - how grateful I am! He Knew I needed each member of your family. You were like a Sister - Most of all you helped lead me to Jesus. "I have a Joy down in my heart."

I Love you forever, Elizabeth Ann

I love you with all my heart.

P.S. I am sending a package with writing + a gift next week.

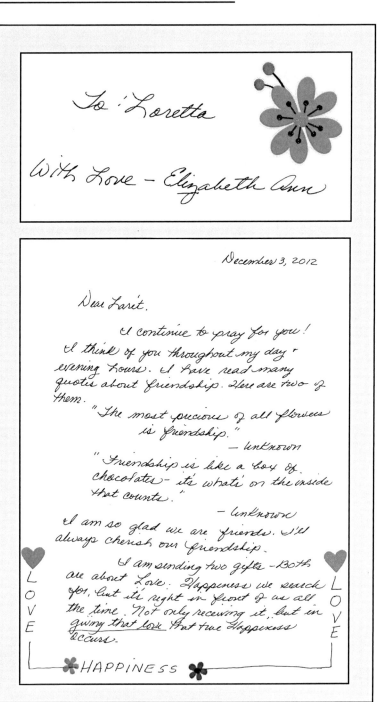

To: Loretta

With Love — Elizabeth Ann

December 3, 2012

Dear Laret,

I continue to pray for you!
I think of you throughout my day &
evening hours. I have read many
quotes about friendship. Here are two of
them.
"The most precious of all flowers
is friendship."
— Unknown

"Friendship is like a box of
chocolates — it's what's on the inside
that counts."
— Unknown
I am so glad we are friends. I'll
always cherish our friendship.
I am sending two gifts — Both
are about Love. Happiness we search
for, but its right in front of us all
the time. Not only receiving it, but in
giving that love that true Happiness
occurs.

L
O
V
E

L
O
V
E

HAPPINESS

84

Letters from Our Best Friends

②

    It takes a long time to write letters, but therapy helps a lot. I hope to write and write again — just like I used to do in school. But writing is improving.

    I appreciate the beautiful postcard. The scenery must have been absolutely gorgeous! — Especially as seen with your family — especially, especially with your wonderful grandchildren.

    I will write to you again soon.
If you want to call, my phone number is   Mary Louise's number is

        I Love You Very Much,
            Elizabeth Ann

Letters from Our Best Friends

November 30, 2012

Dearest Larit,

I can see you now with rolled-up blue jeans dancing + jumping with excitement! How you loved to sing openly, songs about Jesus! How You excited my young spirit and made me yearn for that same kind of vitality and love that you possessed! "Oh How I love Jesus because He first loved me." I began to grasp that He is our Father, That He is the ultimate love."

Greenlaw is part of us. We shared so much. You would come down to my front yard and play Swing the Statue and Red Rover with us. At one of Eddie's birthday parties, you show me how to fix my hands correctly as you passed the Thimble in the game — Thimble-Thimble. You played "Chopsticks" and "Heart and Soul" with me on your piano. Thank you so much for being there for me! Eddie and I played so much. We would tie up my doll like we were playing cowboys and Indians. We took my play pots and pans, started a small fire in our "Hideout" behind bushes in your backyard and heated Thanksgiving dinner. We ate it together! Mimmaw and Uncle Bob's house was right next to us. WoW!!!

Christmas was fun when I came down to see what everyone in your home had gotten. I was <u>always</u> welcome! Your mom was <u>so</u> loving!

Your Dad took my training wheels off my first bike and showed me how to ride it.

Your house was not just a house it was always <u>home</u>! You were blessed with a family who loved one another. Eddie told me when he took me to my senior prom "How much I love my parents and Laritta!" We talked a lot that night about home and family and growing up.

"Today is the gift"
"Yesterday is history — Tomorrow is a mystery. Today is the present — That's why we call it the <u>gift</u>!"

Love You Sweetie!
Elizabeth Oven

A Grandchild Bright and Beautiful

A grandchild is so bright and
   beautiful
Each in his own special way.

- a certain smile
- a tilt of his head
- a sparkle in his eyes

All give you a special knowledge
and feeling that you are part of these
beautiful childrens' being here. Their dad
is your son! You are their grandmother.!!!!

Certainly each child - deep in his heart
and mind - knows the kindness and
loving heart you possess.

Grandmother is so special!
She loves me very much.
Grandmother, with her happy smiles
  and hugs,
Loves me with her every word and touch.

Her heart leaps up when she sees me,
Her spirit is lifted high!
I see her smile so excited.
Her love for me makes HER cry.

Letters from Our Best Friends

A Grandchild Bright and Beautiful
-cont-

She loves me with a love
that is just so much more
than she can hold inside.
Grandmother loves me with
her beautiful soul
Such love overflowing — one that
she cannot hide!

No one is so special in a child's life
as the wonderful loving grandmother that
you are, Loretta! Each child has an individual
knowledge of you, from you only. For a child
listens carefully, observes closely, but most
of all <u>loves</u> completely on his own!

I know that having time with your son +
grandchildren was so precious to you.
I love you!

Elizabeth Ann

Letters from Our Best Friends

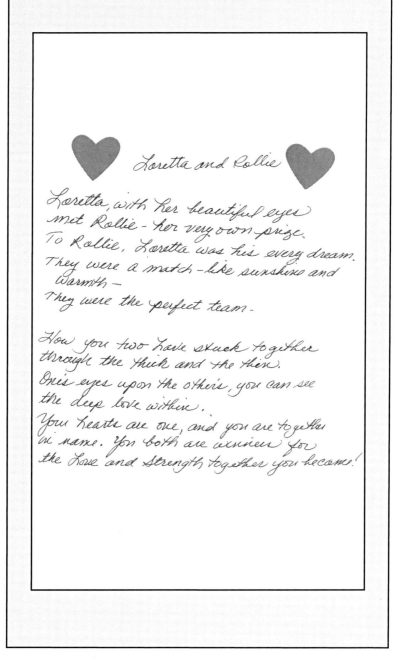

Loretta and Rollie

Loretta, with her beautiful eyes
met Rollie - her very own prize.
To Rollie, Loretta was his every dream.
They were a match - like sunshine and
warmth -
They were the perfect team.

How you two have stuck together
through the thick and the thin.
One's eyes upon the other's, you can see
the deep love within.
Your hearts are one, and you are together
in name. You both are winners for
the Love and Strength, together you became!

Love you, always,
Elizabeth Ann

All Things Beautiful

All things bright and beautiful,
All creatures great and small,
All things wise and wonderful—
The Lord God made them all.

Each little flower that opens,
Each little bird that sings—
He made their glowing colors,
He made their tiny wings.

The purple-headed mountain,
The river running by,
The morning and the sunset
That lighteth up the sky;

The tall trees in the greenwood,
The pleasant summer sun,
The ripe fruits in the garden—
He made them every one.

He gave us eyes to see them,
And lips, that we might tell
How great is God Almighty,
Who hath made all things well.

Cecil Francis Alexander

February 13, 2013

Dear Doug,

I grew up with your mom. She was about 8½ when I met her, and I was around 6. We grew up on Greenlaw Street in North Memphis. She was so full of life! I can see her now with her beautiful red hair, sparkling eyes, T-shirt, rolled-up blue jeans + tennis shoes. She was bouncy — energetic — she radiated! Your mom grew big in the Lord + she overflowed to all of us.

Loretta took an interest in the children in the neighborhood. She was a part of us, and she taught us much, guided us when we needed it. She would join all the kids in our games like "Swing the Statue" and "Red Rover." — Keeping us happy + busy! She taught me many songs like "Do Lord." Also, she taught me how to play "Heart and Soul" on her piano.

Loretta, Eddie, and their mom and dad were "The Family" on Greenlaw — who loved us so — always a piece of cake or a cup of Kool-aid — a welcome home — people who would listen, give a hug to us — + even give good advice.

Loretta was such a big influence in my journey to Getting to Know Jesus! I wanted what she had! — a passion for loving her Lord. That passion energized her — made her jump for joy!

She would come home from Church trips jumping, singing, running toward home — "Do Lord, Oh Do Lord, or Do You Remember Me?" I wanted that Kind of spirit!

Words are inadequate to explain how wonderful Loretta was Because You Know — You are her Son! — Her legacy — HerHeart. She will be a part of you forever!

Love,
Elizabeth Ann

Letters from Our Best Friends

2-13-13

Dear Doug,

Your Mom will be with you—

in spirit and inheart

forever

With Sympathy
Love,
Elizabeth Ann

Letters from Our Best Friends

February 13, 2013

Dear Rollie,

How Special She Was — is !!
Loretta lives on in all of us. She had
an immense spirit! — Enough to share
with anyone and everyone.

She shared most of her life
with you, Rollie - "the Love of my Life!"
So you know just what a Beautiful and
Wonderful person she was.

Loretta was an integral part
of my childhood, therefore influencing
many aspects of my childhood and
adult life — especially her passion for
the Lord! Her excitement about life —
with Christ was immeasurable.

Oh How she loved you! She
expressed this the last time I talked
with her. How many wonderful times you
had shared and what you meant to one
another. Loretta lives on in your memories —
in your spirit & in your heart. Love,
Elizabeth Ann

Letters from Our Best Friends

"Mrs. Robertson"

On Greenlaw – she was the "neatest" mom on the street.
She was in her kitchen – I can see her now making koolaid and icing cake for all of us to eat.
She took us for rides, to the park, and to the store.
She was happy and laughed – I can hear her now sitting in the corner chair by the window
near the dining room door.
She kept us in line – I can feel her concern as she corrected Eddie and me when we did
something wrong with the chemistry set.
She was good and kind – the sweetest personality within of any person you've ever met.
She gave of herself to others you see, and memories galore she gave to me.

Thank you, Mrs. Robertson!
Love, Elizabeth Ann Gullatt-Perry

"God needed an angel in heaven so He took your dear mother home. But she is only as far
away as your heart and lives on as before in your love."

"Eddie"

Eddie was my playmate. We did so many things together. When we flew kites, climbed
trees, hid in the gutter, had leaf tumbles in the Fall, built snowmen in the Winter. We even
dug a hole in your backyard trying to find "hell". Your Dad really got on to us and made us
fill in the hole.

We walked fences, rode bikes, walked to the stores on Jackson Avenue and played cowboys
and Indians. We went trick or treating on Halloween and shared our presents on Christmas.

For my senior prom, Eddie was my date. He was dressed in suit and tie and had a flower for
me. We laughed, talked, sang songs together to the radio in his car. Afterward-dancing for
hours at the prom. Eddie took me to breakfast. What a wonderful time we had!

This beautiful man was such a part of my growing-up days, and I will hold within my heart
memories of my dear friend.

Love, Elizabeth Ann Gullatt-Perry

B. Letters from Our Family

Hi Uncle Rollie,
Glad you are staying busy with the book. I am sending my excerpt and picture in this email. It is hard to sum it all up, but I want you and everyone reading the book to know the lasting imprint that Aunt Loretta left with me and the things I admired in her.

MY LETTER TO AUNT LORETTA

My fondest memories of her in childhood are of opening her thoughtful and creatively wrapped gifts for birthdays and Christmas year after year. She was always so sweet to hand make something and was never late in sending things so that they would arrive with the right momentum for special events. She was the Aunt that you always knew cared for you precisely because of these consistent, thoughtful gestures of her love. I have very vivid memories of dresses, purses, jewelry, scarves, and other "girly" gifts that she endulged us (and I think secretly herself) in. Being that she had one precious son, but no daughters, I think Ericka and I were her escape for creating from her feminine side. As a mom of two boys, I now understand this to a great degree!

Other than her creativity, I most remember her for her adventurous and fun loving side. She was an inspiration to never stop exploring and she loved and appreciated God's creations more than anyone I've ever met. From birds to flowers to mountains, to artisans themselves, aunt Loretta was able to appreciate the details. I find myself to be such a big picture person that I often glaze right over the special reminders God sends when he "winks" at you. She was great at picking up on these precious details in life and I am trying to remember to do this more often in her memory.

As an adult, I came to appreciate her and the dignity and courage she displayed as she fought the final battle for her life her on earth. She told me toward the end, that she wasn't afraid to die, just a little nervous about the process of death itself. Even when she was in great pain in her final day, she was determined to not be "pitiful" she was a picture of courage and strength that I will remember on days when I am weak. I was with her and saw her take her last breath. It was a breath of peace, not of regret nor pain.

I was blessed by my Aunt both through her life and in her death. She was a picture of God's grace and hope for this life and the next.

I Love You,
Meredith 3-27-13

Meredith Claire Robertson Layton

Letters from Our Family

Letter from Ericka:

When I think about my Aunt Loretta, I often think about the things we have in common. From a very early age, I always knew to tell inquirers that I got my red hair from my "Aint Retta." Being the only redhead in an immediate family of brunettes, I was frequently asked where I got my hair color. I was often mistaken as Loretta's daughter instead of her niece, and I was always proud that we shared that unique quality with each other. My Aunt Loretta was one of the most creative people I have ever known, and I like to think that I also inherited some of my "crafty" creativity from her. While I didn't get an inkling of her impressive seamstress abilities, I did end up loving all things kitchen and will never forget her handmade butter mints for Little Mama's 100th birthday party and the Mount St. Helen's mini frosting volcanoes she made for Doug's birthday in Memphis. Her precision and detail-orientation were remarkable, and her flawless handiwork was a direct representation of those qualities. I think Aunt Loretta and I also shared a bit of a red-headed temper at times, but I need not remind anyone of that. :)

Some of my most significant memories lie in the thoughtful gifts she would make for us or bring us from trips she and Uncle Rollie took. Sometimes they would arrive as a parcel crafted from a cereal box turned inside out or would be color coded according my and my sister's preference (I was usually hunter green and sis was red). I have countless scarves that were gifts from her that I will always cherish because she crocheted them herself and wanted us girls to have them. I will certainly miss her and her ingenuity but I know that her legacy will live on through her memoirs, thanks to her passion for and love of history and genealogy.

With much love,

Ericka

Ericka Leigh Robertson Frank

Letters from Our Family

my dearest Loretta   in my prayers!

I am constantly keeping both you and Kellie/ I wanted to send you a note to tell you just how very important you have been in my life. You have been like the big sister I never had. I have always so adored you. I can still remember treasuring you and jewelry you would give me to play with, watching you put on make-up and thinking it had a princess for a cousin! I remember you giving it little Lolita wings when you were a 2-year-old and I thought it was so special. Hearing about the exciting places you went awoke in me a desire to see those places too. When I went to Paris for the first time, I thought about you and everytime I get to see a new place, I am reminded how you awoke that desire to see it all!

As I grew older and saw how creative you were, I felt like I had a kindred spirit and I wanted to be like to make things just like you. Anytime I make anything that is crochet, knit, sewn or put together to create a work of art, you will be with me. Of course, I'm sure you could have done it better ☺

We are so alike you and I - that in our desire to know it, see it or figure out how to do it. To pour over the maps, learn the history and really experience the adventure, sharing those kinds of conversations with you has been one of my deepest treasures.

Both you and Kellie have been a source of strength and comfort to me many times and you have filled a special place in my heart since my beloved parents went to their reward as mine will be one day.

I've watched you struggle with their illness with grace and strength and all the while maintaining that trace of humor I love so much. I am inspired by you and your faith and it deepens my own.

You have always been so good and kind to me, I'm so glad after I knew you got to see me married to someone who really makes me happy ☺

You are the most beautiful, talented, smart and courageous person I know and you will live in my heart forever.

Both Jared and I are here for both you and Kellie. I treasure our little big brother and there is nothing I wouldn't do for you.

You are loved and cherished and your life has been a huge success. I am so very fortunate to have you to emulate.

...but how
do you mail
a hug?

I love you!

Karen

I'm sticking in my card with all our numbers if there is anything I can do for either one of you.

Take care and we are sending love —
Your little Cuz

Karen Allen Alvarado

Letters from Our Family

April 3, 2013

Dear Loretta,

I enjoyed so much the months that we were able to talk on the phone about the great times that we had when we were growing up. Our special ones were always the wonderful family picnics that we had at Overton Park with all the food that everyone brought and celebrated Grandma's (Gurley) birthday. I remember the time when we had five generations there together at one time which was so very unique and wonderful.

I appreciate the pictures that you found that I was in as well as the others that you sent to me; some I had actually forgotten. I appreciate the older ones of you and your family. I love all the older pictures of all our families. The most meaningful again would be the one taken at Overton Park. Overton Park was a great place to go back then. I also played in the summer band headed by Roy Coates of Humes High School each summer with the rehearsals held at Humes High School. Each Sunday afternoon in the summer we held a concert in the pavilion at Overton Park. Guess that is just another reason it is special to me.

I was always so glad that you could talk to me about your illness and so openly and freely about everything and I never tired of listening to you. You always told me about yours and Rollie's trip out west and the little store where you bought your yarn. I never knew what you were making with it at the time. I was just so glad that you were able to make as many trips as you did that you seemed to enjoy so very much.

I remember going to your birthday party one year on Greenlaw . I could not have been more than four years old, but I do remember going and eating the best" chocolate cake" ever. I know that your mother made this as I remember her just finishing up the frosting when we came in. I remember spending one night with you there on Greenlaw and reading comic books: "Little Lulu" and also "Archie." I recall the visits that my family made on Sunday afternoons with your family. They were all so nice, and I remember them like they were only yesterday.

I haven't forgotten spending the night with you a night or two when you all moved and we played in a little playhouse Uncle Douglas had made for you and fighting the "chiggers."

Well, we reached high school age and I remember a boy that I was dating had a friend that had come into town one week-end and needed a date so that we could double-date. I called you, and you accepted, and we all went to the movies in one of the big movie theaters in downtown Memphis at that time. All I remember was that it was a good movie, but, back then, ALL movies were" GOOD" movies.

As time went on and we graduated from high school we pretty much lost touch as we tried to make a future for ourselves. I was only able to be with you at the birthdays that we had for Mammaw (Little Mama), and we all were able to talk a little and have a good time.

I guess life is mostly made of "Memories" and our family had some very nice ones. It helps to think back on the good times in life as I think you always do as well as I do myself.

Letters from Our Family

Included is a picture of Doug and myself. This one is the most recent that we have. We were just leaving to go to my 50th high school reunion. I was just 17 when I graduated. I started school when I was only five. My birthday being in December made you and me 2 ½ years apart in age with yours being in June. You mentioned that when daddy was in the navy gone on the ship during the war that somewhere that the ship docked he bought you something and sent it to you. He also bought me a grass skirt and I have included a picture with me in it when we lived on Barrett St. (Just more great "memories.")

In fact, with yours and my daddy's birthday being on the same day, June 12th, our daughter, Kimberly, chose June 12th, 2010 as her wedding day and wore both her grandmothers' wedding rings on her right hand. I was very impressed that family meant that much to her. It is nice to pass on something very valuable down to the next generation. I hope the "now generations" of our family will find and enjoy some of the "simple" things in life as we did so many, many years ago. Those are the real treasures of life that no one can ever take away!

Love,

Jerry Anne Starnes
(Your 1st cousin)

Jerry Anne Jones Starnes

Letters from Our Family

Doug Riesberg

Letter to my Mother (Mom), 7/23/13

My mom was different in that she had "Red Hair", was white as snow) except for a few freckles here & there), had a great sense of humor & wit about her, knew a lot about most everything & if she didn't, she tried extremely hard to find or figure it out! I loved that she had wisdom & knowledge beyond her years & wasn't afraid to share that with me or anyone else! As I got older & understood more about her, I tried to talk her into being a teacher or share with others her wealth of knowledge, but she'd always humbly tell me "Oh, people don't want to listen to me & I'm too old or can't do that." I was extremely blessed to have her as long as I did! She loved me & life, but mostly importantly, her Savior! She was loving, caring, nurturing, helpful & thoughtful. I will remember the many trips we got to take together around the world, over seas & mountains, under bridges, through meadows, valleys, tunnels & flowered fields, hiking, biking, walking, swimming & vacationing...my Mom loved travelling & living with her family! She was adventurous (like her Father & my Paw Paw) in every moment...thank you Mom, Delta & God for the opportunity to travel & see so many sights God created for our enjoyment & wonderment! Wow, what a life I've had with my Mom! I'll miss your good cookin' & wish I'd spent more time in the kitchen with you really trying to understand & make sense of it all! I remembered a few things you taught me & that I picked up on along the way & even though I don't have your skills, at least I have some of your wonderful recipes you gave me if I need to taste it again once mor... and who knows, if I'd paid better attention, I may have been working alongside cousins Ericka or Meredith in St. Louis or Knoxville at "THE CUP" in the business of making, baking & decorating cakes & cupcakes... hey, at least I can boil some eggs & make a mean "Tuna-Fish Salad" or rustle-up some breakfast cereal!

Mom, thanks for all you selflessly did for me & raised me the way you did...to love & serve others &God! Love you & miss you, until we meet again at them Pearly-Gates, your one & only son...Love , Doug

Letter to and about my Mom   7/23/13

The word or words that come to mind when I think about my Mother (Mom) are Special & Unique! She was in so many ways "Special to me". The way she nurtured & cared for me from infanthood to adulthood. I loved her and miss her "Special " hugs that were heartfelt & fun from the first squeeze! I miss her laughter, zest & zeal for life & living life to the fullest for her Lord & Savior Jesus Christ! She loved us & her family deeply & would do anything for use and anyone without heswitation! She was Uniquely Special & Especially Unique in all that she did, touched, thought, saw, gave & served. The Slogan "Service with a smile" comes to mind. She loved serving & being & took that job seriously & to heart.

Doug Riesberg

Letters from Our Family

Zachary's Letter to Grandma (Maw)

Zachary Douglas Riesberg

My grandmother goes by many names such as; Loretta, Mom, and Aunt Loretta, but to me she will always be Grandmaw. She is the most unique person I have ever known. Every moment I spent with her she was always smiling even when she was in pain. She showed so much strength for somebody facing so much pain which is something special. No matter how much pain she felt she always put on a smile when we (my brothers and I) were around. On one of her last days with us while she was in a coma and we all did not know what would happen, whether we would see another miracle or if Jesus would take her home, all of the fun memories passed through my mind.

When I was younger, my grandparents and I would spend a day together where we would go see a movie and eat dinner afterwards, usually at Krystal's. After dinner we would head back to their house and I would spend the night with them (I would always sleep with Paw because Grandmaw snored like a thunderstorm). The next morning she would make us a five star breakfast to eat. Occasionally, before they took me home, we would go to a park or the library where we would spend a couple of hours.

Another memory we shared were our trips out west. Every few years we would go on a vacation to amazing places including Grand Canyon, Montana, and Utah. I specifically enjoyed some parts of our Utah trip. The most entertaining thing we did was go to a place called Mayan Adventure, a restaraunt with an interactive show. We went there multiple times on our trip because it was so fun. On our trips there were always fun activities planned. Together we shared many great adventures.

Another thing I cherished about her is her personality. She was always easy going and loved to talk and tell stories of nature and her past. She loves to make things, to make things such as scarves and blankets for us and she is an amazing artist. I always enjoy looking at her drawings and I also enjoy watching videos of her as a child and her outgoing character multiplied in her youth.

In her last days when we did not know if she would wake up all of these memories and more flashed through my head while I was holding her hand while we did not know when and if God would take her home to be with Him or if he would give her another miracle as He had many times before in her battle with cancer. We left that night without knowing if we would ever be able to tell her we loved her again. The next day we were notified that she had awoken in the night, so we went hoping to see her again. We spent a couple of hours with her and while we were there I never left her side, wanting to soak in our possible last minutes together. She told me stories of her life and I was so glad God gave her another miracle so we could talk with her and tell her we loved her. Even though we will never see her again in this life I am happy she no longer feels any pain and is at home with her Lord and savior for eternity. I love you grandmaw and can't wait to see you again someday in Heaven.

"Sing to the Lord, you saints of his; praise his holy name. For His anger lasts only a moment, but his favor lasts a lifetime; weeping may remain for a night, but joy comes in the morning." – Plsalm 30:4-5

– Zachary Douglas Riesberg

Letters from Our Family

Jeremiah Riesberg

Jeremiah's Letter to Grandma (Maw)

For I know the plans I have for you says The Lord, plans
not to harm you but to give you a hope and a future:
Jeremiah 29:11.
She was the best grandma anybody could have, she was
NICE, KIND, and most of all CARING. I will never forget
the wonderful moments I had with HER! I love you Maw!
Your grandson,
Jeremiah.

Letters from Our Family

Nathaniel Riesberg

Nathaniel's Letter to Grandma (Maw)

From - Nathaniel   5-13-13

Maw My favorite bible
verse is Genesis 1:1
In the begining Dad
Created the heavens and
the earth. I remember her
red hair, beautiful Glasses, the way
she dressed, and the trips she
made

Letters from Our Family

Ethan's Letter to Grandma (Maw)

Ethan Riesberg

you are my favorite
person and you are
the kindest person
in the world,

My favorite bible verse
is John 3:16 For god so
loved the world in his way:
he gave his one and only
son so that everyone
who believes in him will
not perish but have a
eternal life.

The Day Loretta Came Out of the Coma

The Day before Loretta Went to Heaven

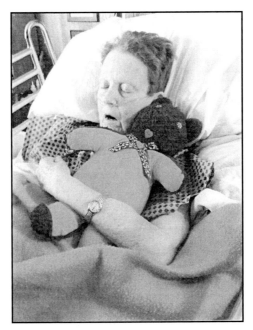

Poem : I Did Not Die

I DID NOT DIE

Do not stand at my grave and weep;

I am not there. I do not sleep.

I am a thousand winds that blow.

I am the diamond glints on snow.

I am the sunlight on a ripened grain.

I am the gentle autumn's rain.

When you awaken in the morning's hush,

I am the swift uplifting rush

of quiet birds in circled flight.

I am the soft stars that shine at night.

Do not stand at my grave and cry;

I am not there. I did not die.

Unknown

Song : Now I Belong to Jesus

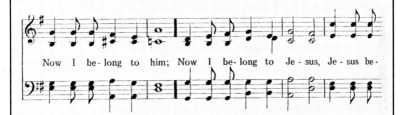

Now I be-long to him; Now I be-long to Je-sus, Je-sus be-

Loretta & Rollie – Happy and At Peace (Grand Canyon November 2012)

C. Loretta's Last Delta Flight

DL 1281 Tuesday Feb. 12, 2013
Left Atlanta 13:50 pm – Arrived Memphis 14:19pm
DL 777 Tuesday Feb. 12, 2013
Left Memphis 14:19 p.m. – Arrived Heaven for
Eternity

Our precious Loretta, we love and miss you so very much! You changed our lives!
We are eagerly looking forward to being with you in Heaven with Jesus and God!

CHAPTER 10.

The Best Phase of My Life----- Witnessing for God

God loves me and has been so very good to me and my family----I want to tell others about how much He loves all of us. He loves us so very much that He sent His only begotten Son, Jesus Christ to this world to die for us and our sins (John 3:16).

God Loves You

God loves you just the way you are, but He loves you too much to let you stay that way. God does not change us so that He can love us, He loves us so that He can change us. God is a God of new, fresh beginnings!

I know that I have grown and matured in my spiritual life because there is nothing in this world that gives me more happiness than sharing God's love for me with other people. God loves each and every one of us equally and without limits. The closer we are to Him, the closer He will be to us. When we 'hold our guard up' and push Him away through our sinful ways, without repenting of our sins, we don't let Him get closer to us. With this I pray, "Dear God, please help me keep the devil away from my heart and off my back." We must repent of our sins and turn our lives over to God completely. If you will let God come into your heart, there is nothing that will fulfill you more and make you happier than witnessing for Him.

In February of last year (2013), God brought my precious wife, Loretta home to Heaven to be with Him. She battled dreadful cancer for 4 years and 10 months. Since then, I have asked God in my many prayers and discussions with Him, "Why didn't You bring me home when You brought my dear Loretta home?" He told me that He has a lot of work for me to do for Him and with Him-----He wants my life to count for something---Him and me!" Dear God, I know the only way I am going to make it through is by serving You!

What makes me happiest of all and keeps me going with my deeply broken heart from my loss of my precious Loretta, is my witnessing for God, telling everyone about how very much God loves them. Love is the best thing in the world and a bro-ken heart is the worst. God brought Loretta home to Heaven on Delta Air Lines Flight 777 to keep her from suffering any longer and too, He needed another angel to help Him. Loretta got cancer because of sin in the world. God removed her from the cancer, giving her restful peace in Heaven. I am living for the day when I can join God, Jesus and Loretta in Heaven, but until that day, I have a lot of work to do and a golden opportunity to serve our Heavenly Father, witnessing and sharing my life's story with others.

WITNESSING: To help you, I want you to know: You Are Loved and You Can Do Great Things With Your Life!!

You are Loved and You Can Do
Great Things With Your Life
(God is Love: Beloved, if God so loved us,
we ought also to love one another.)
(1 John 4:11)

Make your life count for something...........count for God and you!

DAWNING OF A NEW DAY

New Hope Baptist Church
Fayetteville, GA

© 2014 ROLLAND RIESBERG

God wants us to use the blessings He has given us (our talents, our intelligence, our knowledge and our time) to His and our best advantage to the glory of His kingdom. We must use our many blessings to help our fellowman, ourselves and to serve God the way He intended.

God loves you just the way you are, but He loves you too much to let you stay that way. God does not change us so that He can love us, He loves us so that He can change us. God is a God of new, fresh beginnings.

In life, God wants us to work hard, yearn to learn and in your journey with Him, place your total faith and trust in Him and He will lead you all the way to help you achieve great things for you and for Him. He loves you so much, He sent His Son, Jesus Christ to die for your sins, that you may have eternal life. Jesus died in your place and your sin debt has been paid-in-full by His blood on the cross.
Pray to God and thank Him!!!

New Hope Baptist Church
551 New Hope Road
Fayetteville, GA 30214
(770) 461-4337
www.newhopebc.org

CHAPTER 11.

Tribute to Our Lord and Savior, Jesus Christ

We are all so very blessed to have Jesus as the foundation and capstone of our lives!

Without Him, we could not have been able to get through the loss of our dear loved ones. Through our love, faith and trust in Jesus, our Lord and Savior, we know that our loved ones, who have passed from this earthly home, are resting peaceful and pain free, eternally with Him in Heaven. Thank you God, for that assurance!

Loretta's favorite bible verse has always been the 23rd Psalm.

The Lord is my shepherd, I shall not want.
He maketh me to lie down in green pastures,
he leads me beside the still waters,
he restoreth my soul:
He leadeth me in paths of righteousness for his name's sake.
Yea, though I walk through the valley of the shadow of death,
I will fear no evil, for thou art with me;
thy rod and thy staff, they comfort me.
Thou preparest a table before me
in the presence of mine enemies:
thou anointest my head with oil; my cup runneth over.
Surely goodness mercy shalll follow me all the days of my life,
and I will dwell in the house of the Lord for ever.

Rollie's favorite bible verses are Luke 23:46 and John 3:16.

- And when Jesus had cried with a loud voice, he said, Father, into thy hands I commend my spirit: and having said thus; he gave up the ghost.

- For God so loved the world, that he gave his only begotten Son, that whosoever believeth in him should not perish, but have everlasting life.

Doug's favorite bible verse is Isaiah 53:5 ASV; and Hebrews 12:28-29.

"Therefore, since we are receiving a kingdom
that cannot be shaken,
let us be thankful, and so worship God acceptably
with reverence and awe,
for our 'God is a consuming fire'."

God called Loretta home to Heaven on February 7, 2013. She fought dreadful cancer for over 4 ½ years, having 4 surgeries (colon/rectal, lung and abdominal) and numerous chemotherapy and radiation treatments over that period of time. Her pain levels ranged from moderate to heavy, and excruciating at times, especially during her last 3 months of life. Our hearts are broken------but we are very happy that she is in Heaven with Jesus and God no longer suffering.

Loretta and I thought God had given her several miracles during the almost 5 year period and we were fervently praying for another one so she could have time to finish her 'Story-of-Her-Life-As-a- Christian witnessing book for God'.......*God Bless the Moon and God Blessed Me*. Obviously, God needed her to come home sooner to keep her from suffering any longer; also He wanted me to finish her book for her and Him.

God, we also want to thank You for preparing us and the rest of our family and friends for Loretta's soon imminent journey to Heaven. You allowed her to go into a coma on January 28 and 29, since the cancer had spread to her liver. Then, with Doug, Ericka and I in the room sitting next to her, on January 30 at 3:00 am, You gave her another miracle where she fully regained consciousness and alertness so that she could be released from the hospice facility 3 days later on February 2, to return home into a hospital-type bed. Her miraculous semi-recovery gave us more time with her and helped lessen the heartache of us losing her in the earthly form 5 days later.

Doug and I are eternally grateful to Loretta for her Christian influence in keeping our family deeply grounded in our faith and trust in Jesus as our Lord and Savior. Loretta brought me to Jesus when I was 27 years old, a year after we married. When we got married in July of 1964, we made a commitment to God and one another where we were joined together by heart, mind and soul. That commitment will never be broken!

Now, Doug and his wife, Amy and I are committed to teaching their 4 precious boys (and my grandsons) to grow up loving Jesus.

Thank You, God for giving us Your Son Jesus Christ to die for our sins, for giving us the many pleasures, opportunities and good times of our lives; for getting us through the pain and suffering and bad times. This is not a sad ending but a new, happy beginning for all of us.

Rollie
(devoted husband)

Doug
(devoted son)

SPECIAL SECTION

A. Family Personal Profiles

NOTE: Please take the time to read the Family Personal Profiles to learn from life experiences and how to better cope with difficult situations in your own life.

(1) Rolland (Rollie) George Riesberg
-Born May 8, 1938 Tulsa, Oklahoma (Morningside Hospital)
-Parents: Ralph Orlin Riesberg and Mayme (Mae) Mary Moore Riesberg
-Nationality: Swedish, Norwegian, Irish & French

-Personality: Rollie has always been an affectionate, ambitious, determined, trustworthy, hard-working, intelligent, caring person wanting other people to like him. It bothered him when he felt someone didn't like him.

He continuously strove for perfection at anything he chose to undertake. Perhaps this came from him always wanting to please and make his Dad proud of him. Rollie can be quite stubborn, but many times that has worked to his advantage. Sometimes it can take longer for him to get over "being mad"---that could be where the stubbornness works to his disadvantage.

Rollie has always been industrious, wanting to make money---maybe that comes from the childhood no-money, hungry years. Rollie started working for money at the age of 7. Like most kids, he had a newspaper route. In the summer after completing the 6th grade of school, he had a job washing dishes (by hand) in a split-sink with a drip-dry tray for a local drive-in café. During his teenage years, Rollie worked as a cleaner/stock-boy for a local drug store, stocker/delivery boy for a local grocery store, and later on, a cashier/stocker for a major super market chain. After graduating from high school (Daniel Webster), since there was no money for college, Rollie joined the U.S. Air Force for 4 years where he became a Jet Mechanic working on B-47 Bomber aircraft assigned to Strategic Air Command at Chennault Air Force Base in Lake Charles, LA. After being Honorably Discharged from the Air Force, Rollie worked for 2 months for Santa Fe Railroad/Truck Lines loading and unloading trucks and trains; the work was hard but the pay was excellent. However, Rollie wanted a college degree more than life itself, so he left for college at the end of summer.

That September of 1960, Rollie moved to Shreveport, Louisiana where he enrolled at Centenary College (he finally had money for college). His Uncle George was gracious enough to let Rollie live with him and his newly wed wife, Billye during the first semester until he had time to find a place of his own. Rollie worked for Kroger as a cashier/stocker, part time, until he was hired by Delta Air Lines as a full time Ramp Service Agent in January of 1961. There at Delta, in that same year, is where he met "the love of his life", Laurie Robertson, a lovely, tall, red-headed Stewardess, who was working her 3rd Flight (a Convair 440 aircraft) from Memphis to Houston via Shreveport. It must have been "love at first sight" because up until then, Rollie did not like "red-heads".

This "life-time romance" started out with Rollie and Laurie becoming best friends. They shared common interests and goals, likes and dislikes, and most important of all, they communicated very well with each other---sharing innermost thoughts and feelings. Laurie was the easiest person to talk with Rollie had ever met---and the most compassionate. Anyway, this "best friendship" gradually started blossoming into a "life-time romance", even though at first, it was a <u>long distance</u> romance with Rollie in Shreveport and Laurie in Memphis. (They were miserable when they were apart!) So---the logical thing to do about the situation was for Rollie to change colleges, to a better school, Memphis State University, as long as he could get a transfer with Delta from Shreveport to Memphis (which he did in April of 1964). Rollie attended classes for the first summer session at Memphis State but did not attend the second session---he and Laurie had a "big" wedding to attend (their own) on July 24, 1964. (They honeymooned in Hawaii, compliments of Delta Air Lines, Pan American Airways and Rollie's Dad (most expenses paid). <u>NOTE</u>: Regarding the Marriage: Laurie assured Rollie that she would <u>never</u> do anything to interfere with him getting his College Degree because she knew that "he wanted that degree more than life itself"!

In Memphis, Rollie worked on the ramp full time for Delta while attending college almost full time, just like he did in Shreveport. Three and a half years later, he graduated from Memphis State University with a B.S. Degree in Industrial Engineering. (Now Rollie would <u>never</u> have to fear going hungry again!)

By this time, Rollie already had 7 years seniority with Delta and didn't want to leave and go to work for another company---Delta had been good to him and he appreciated it! Rollie and Laurie (now Loretta) flew to Atlanta on Delta to spend 2 days for Rollie to interview for various jobs (positions available) mostly in the Engineering Department at Delta. After returning to Memphis and waiting until Monday of the following week, Rollie got a phone call from the Engineering Department offering him a choice of 2 positions---he picked the Materials and Processes Engineering position---which turned out to be the best choice, for many reasons.

After many years in the Engineering Department, Rollie decided he wanted to make a career change and try to transfer into the Finance Division at Delta. But he knew that credentials and experience were needed. So, he enrolled in the College for Financial Planning and formed his own part time Financial Planning business, Financial Growth Services. In his first interview in the Investment Management Department which managed the 401(k) Plan at Delta, Rollie was fortunate to place among the top 4 candidates for the position; however, one of the other candidates was ultimately selected. By the time Rollie got into position to become the top candidate for other positions available in the Finance Division, Delta started offering entry-level-like salaries for those positions; he had no choice but to decline the offers because he could not afford the substantial pay-cut.

A few years later, airline prosperity and profits were being strained by the 1990-91 recession and Delta Air Lines had to start cutting costs. The first place on the "cut list" was personnel and salaries. Those employees with 30 or more years seniority were sent letters asking them to take voluntary retirement---with the alternative being, lay-offs and job phase outs, if needed. Anyway, Rollie accepted Delta's offer and retired with almost 32 years service. Rollie retired on Aug. 31, 1992 and went to work for Lockheed Martin in Marietta, GA as a Senior Materials & Processes Engineer on Sept. 1, 1992 (the next day).

Rollie worked for Lockheed Martin for 6 years before deciding to retire again. The Engineering responsibility for the L-1011 and Jet Star aircraft was being transferred from Lockheed-Marietta, GA to Lockheed-Greenville, SC. Lockheed-Greenville Management found out that Rollie was retiring and made him an offer to be the on-site Materials & Processes Engineer there; FAA (Federal Aviation Agency) requires that an M & P Engineer be on-site where Commercial aircraft are being overhauled, modified and serviced. Rollie accepted the generous offer, on a contractual basis. The contract lasted for a year and a half. Then a direct (not contract) employee, from another company, was found as a replacement for Rollie. (Contract employees are paid much higher wages than direct, salaried employees.) Rollie's replacement had been laid off for 4 months by another aircraft manufacturer and was happy to be offered Rollie's job or any other job---for that matter. The rest is HISTORY.

Now, Rollie needed no more excuses to come <u>full</u> time into his Financial Planning business. This was one of the <u>BEST</u> decisions he ever made in his life---because this is a "people <u>helping</u> people" business.

-Best Job: His Ramp Service Agent job with Delta in Shreveport where God used Delta to bring Laurie and Rollie together. He and Laurie are eternally grateful to God and Delta for that "Golden Opportunty" of their lives.

-Worst Job: Dishwasher for Drive-in Café; Twenty-eight straight days of KP (pots & pans) while in the Air Force; (tie).

(2) <u>Loretta (Laurie) Claire Robertson</u>
<u>Riesberg</u>
-Born June 12, 1941 Memphis, Tennessee
(Methodist Hospital)
-Parents: Douglas Edward Robertson, Sr.
and Marietta Jones Robertson
-Nationality: Scotch, Cherokee Indian,
Welsh & Irish

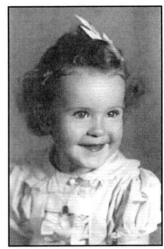

-Personality: Loretta has always been an affectionate, caring, dedicated, talented, trustworthy, intelligent, hard-working person wanting other people to like her. It bothered her when she felt someone didn't like her. She was always trying to give of herself to entertain and try to make other people happy. As a Flight Attendant (Stewardess) for Delta Air Lines, whenever she had an unhappy passenger on her flight, she felt like it was up to her to make him/her happy---and by the time the aircraft landed, thanks to Loretta's finesse and people skills, most of the passengers had forgotten just what it was that made them mad or unhappy in the first place. (They got off of the aircraft in a good mood and feeling happy.)

This deep-seated desire for Loretta to want people to like and love her began with her Daddy, Mother and Brother. For her Daddy, it was harder for him to show approval and acceptance for anyone (not just his Wife, Daughter and Son).

Loretta always worked hard and endeavored to do her very best at any job or anything she chose to undertake. Not counting selling Gordon's potato chips and delivering Telephone Directory books (with Daddy and Mother's help) as a preteen girl, Loretta as a teenager, had a part time job working at a local movie theater. One memorable occasion was when a little boy brought his bag of popcorn back to the Concession Stand complaining that there was a cockroach in his popcorn; a co-worker replied to the little boy, "If you don't stop complaining, we will charge you extra for the <u>meat</u>!"

Once Loretta graduated from high school (Central High), she started college at Memphis State University in the fall of 1959, majoring in Education. Her parents told her that they would provide her with a car and pay her tuition if she would continue living at home and attend a local college; of course, she agreed. To help out with all of the expenses of attending college, Loretta got a part time job working for a family friend, Bill Phillips, who owned and operated Phillips Property & Casualty insurance agency.

Two years have now passed; Loretta is mid-way through college and has 2 years experience working for Mr. Phillips as his secretary. (This is where God's Divine Providence begins.) One day in early June of 1961, when there wasn't much work to be done at the Agency, Mr. Phillips told Loretta, "Why don't you take the afternoon off!" Loretta replied, "Why? I don't have anything else to do. Where would I go?" Mr. Phillips reply was, "Well, why not drive out to the airport and watch the airplanes take off?" Loretta said, "Okay" and left for the airport. Once there, Loretta parked her car and entered the terminal. Not knowing what to do or see first, she stopped at the Delta Air Lines ticket counter. An agent looked up at Loretta and asked, "Can I help you?" Loretta said, "Well---I don't know." He said, "I'll bet you are here to apply for a Stewardess position." Loretta's eyes all of a sudden lit up, and she replied, "Well---I guess so." He directed her to the Stewardess office, where she filled out an Application for Employment and took a couple of tests. While there at the airport that afternoon, Loretta figured that she might as well go ahead and complete Applications for Stewardess positions with American Airlines and United Air Lines. Within a week, Loretta had been flown to Atlanta, GA by Delta for another interview and more testing; having been selected for that position, she started Stewardess class in Atlanta the next week. Two weeks later, American Airlines contacted Loretta for an interview; the next week after that, United

Air Lines also called her. Of course, she thanked them for their interest in her but declined because she had already been hired by Delta. (Now, how is that for God leading us and working in our lives!) If Loretta had been hired by American of United instead of Delta, we would have <u>never</u> met.

I thank God for bringing Loretta to me! She has been my best friend confidant, life-long loving companion and my inspiration. She has been so loving and understanding and easy to love. She represents to me, everything my childhood life was not. She has given me someone to share my dreams with and has given me a wonderful son to love, as well.

-Best Job: Stewardess for Delta Air Lines
-Worst Job: none.

(3) <u>Doug Riesberg</u>
-Parents: Rolland George Riesberg and
Loretta Claire Robertson Riesberg
-Nationality: Swedish, Norwegian, Irish,
French, Scotch, Cherokee Indian &
Welsh

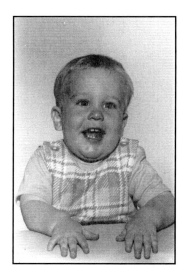 

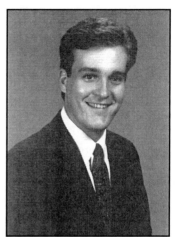

-Personality: Doug has always been an affectionate, caring, trustworthy, talented, dedicated, outgoing, intelligent, hard-working person wanting other people to like him. It bothers him when he feels someone doesn't like him. As a child, teenager and young adult, Doug was always trying to entertain others and make them happy. He is always putting others first before himself. Doug has always strived for perfection on anything he endeavored to do; that probably comes from having "perfectionist" parents. (And naturally, striving for perfection takes longer to get tasks accomplished.)

Doug's parents were by no means perfect but they earnestly strived to provide him with a better home (economically, physically and spiritually) than what they had as children. Most importantly, Doug was raised and taught to love Jesus as his Lord and Savior and to attend church regularly.

Like most children approaching their teens, Doug started his working years making extra "money of his own" mowing lawns and washing & waxing cars. During the later teen years, Doug worked various summer jobs which included: 1) Movie Theater Usher 2) Nursery Commercial Business Landscaper 3) Passenger Assist Agent for then, Eastern Air Lines, along with his best friend, Ryan McDonald and 4) A Disk Jockey for a local Christian Radio Station, WSSA.

Doug's main hobby and interest during Junior High and High School was playing in the High School Concert and Marching Bands. Doug's parents provided Drum lessons for him from school grades 7 through 12. Of course, Doug was the Drummer for several Christian Rock bands during those later school years and after graduation from High School. With all of his music experience and talent, Doug was able to get his own Christian Rock Music Show which he named, White Metal Explosion as a Disk Jockey at WSSA, 1570 AM.

During the "after high school" years, Doug transitioned through various airline jobs including: 1) AMR Services (American Airlines) working as a Ticket Agent contractor for Air Jamaica and Sabena airlines 2) Value Jet/Air Tran airlines as a Gate Agent, and eventually,

3) Delta Air Lines as a Ramp Service Agent, and then 2 years later, GateAgent, a position he now holds.

I thank God for giving me my Son, Doug. I have always wantcd Doug and I to have a very strong Father/Son relationship. I am very proud of him and I love him so very much!

-Best Job: Disk Jockey/Drummer in Christian Rock Band/His present Gate Agent position (3 way tie)
-Worst Job: Working for a nursery as a commercial business landscaper.

(4) <u>Amy Garrett Riesberg</u>
-Parents: Rodney Garrett and Kathy Daily
-Nationality: unknown

-Personality: Amy is an intelligent, hard-working, complex, more reserve person. She has a strong allegiance to her family. She loves our Son, Doug and our four Grandsons (Zachary, Jeremiah, Nathaniel and Ethan) very much. She strives for perfection on anything she endeavors to accomplish.

As a child starting Elementary school, she wasn't happy going to a Public school; so from then on, her parents enrolled her in a Private Christian school. The school was samll and each student was able to receive a lot of special teaching and attention from each teacher. Amy's High School Senior Class had 4 graduating seniors (Amy and 3 others, who naturally, were real close).

Not much is known about Amy's other jobs experience. While still in High School, she worked part time in the Payroll Department for John Wieland Homes (once she graduated, she started working full time).

Once Amy and Doug met, they started dating, fell in love and got married. Amy decided that she would only work part time. Consequently, John Wieland had to transfer her to their Home Mortgage Department. Some years later, the Housing Industry fell upon "hard times" and Amy, being a part time employee, was laid off. In the mean time, Amy was able to find part time work at she and Doug's and our Grandson's church, New Hope Baptist as the Children's Sunday School Superintendent. Eventually, Amy was offered a position (part time) in the Corporate Tax Department with Chick-fil-A, a position she now holds.

I love Amy and want to love her like our own Daughter (which we never had).

-Best Job: Chick-fil-A Corporate Tax Specialist
-Worst Job: unknown

(5) <u>Zachary Riesberg</u>
-Parents: Douglas Riesberg and
Amy Garrett Riesberg
-Nationality: Swedish, Norwegian,
Irish, French, Scotch, Cherokee Indian,
Welsh, other

-Personality: Zachary is an
intelligent, caring, loving, more
reserve person. He loves his 3
younger brothers so very much; he
tries to "teach" them and take good
care of them. Zachary loves to read
better than anything and likes

school. He has been an "honors student" for a numbers of years now.

Being the tallest in his class at school, when he was a young boy, he played center on the Church Association basketball team.

Zachary is precious to me; I love him and his 3 Brothers very much!

When he was a little boy, he used to love for me, his "Paw", to wrestle him down and and hold him tight in the "Lazy Boy" chair to keep him from escaping jail. If one of his little brothers tagged him, he had to be released from jail.

I thank his Dad and Mom for raising him to love Jesus!

(6) <u>Jeremiah Riesberg</u>
-Parents: Douglas Riesberg and Amy
Garrett Riesberg
-Nationality: Swedish,
Norwegian, Irish, French, Scotch,
Cherokee Indian, Welsh, other

-Personality: Jeremiah is an intelligent, caring, loving, outgoing and lively person. He loves his older brother and 2 younger brothers so very much. He is always trying to entertain them and make them happy. Jeremiah loved to perform and do "Elvis Presley" and other impersonations and do magic tricks. He loves playing outdoors and playing soccer; he was on his Church

Association soccer and basketball teams.

He now loves playing baseball as a pitcher on his Fayette County Youth baseball team. Also, he is a superb artist and loves to draw pictures of everything.

Jeremiah is precious to me; I love him and his 3 Brothers so very much!

I thank his Dad and Mom for raising him to love Jesus!

(7) Nathaniel Riesberg
     -Parents: Douglas Riesberg and
     Amy Garrett Riesberg
      -Nationality: Swedish, Norwegian, Irish,
     French, Scotch, Cherokee Indian,
     Welsh, other

-Personality: Nathaniel is an intelligent, caring, loving, active and outgoing person. He is usually kind to his brothers, letting them "pick first" and have their way. Nathaniel loves his 2 older brothers and younger brother so very much.

He loves to play ball (any kind) and throws very well with either hand (but he writes right-handed). He now plays baseball as a pitcher on his Fayette County Youth baseball team. His is also the "Home Run King".

He is our big-boy "helper"---whatever you are doing at the time, he wants to help you do it (and he does it very well for a little guy).

Nathaniel is precious to me; I love him and his 3 Brothers so very much!

I thank his Dad and Mom for raising him to love Jesus!

(8) <u>Ethan Riesberg</u>
   -Parents: Douglas Riesberg and
   Amy Garrett Riesberg
   -Nationality: Swedish, Norwegian, Irish,
   French, Scotch, Cherokee Indian,
   Welsh, other

-Personality: Ethan is an intelligent, caring, loving, active, outgoing person. He was a very busy little guy, playing with all of his and his brothers' toys. He loved to come to Paw's and Maw's house where their Dad's childhood toys have been saved--- especially for them (all 4 of our Grandsons have loved playing with "Dad's toys"). As do most children, Ethan loves playing outdoors with his 3 older brothers. When he was a little guy, he learned how to manipulate his older brothers to get <u>his</u> way, saying "because I am wittle" (little).

He now plays basketball on our church youth team and he is right in the middle of <u>each</u> play and is always the top scorer. Also, he is an outfielder on his Fayette County Youth baseball team. He is the "Home Run King".

Ethan is precious to me; I love him and his 3 Brothers so very much!

I thank his Dad and Mom for raising him to love Jesus!

(9) <u>Ralph Orlin Riesberg</u>
-Born December 16, 1909 Minneapolis,
Minnesota
-Deceased: July 28, 1978 Kaneohe,
Hawaii
-Parents: August Sigfried Riesberg and
Helga Theresa Moss Riesberg
-Nationality: Swedish, Norwegian

-Personality: Ralph was a caring,
outgoing, intelligent, ambitious, hard-
working, innovative person. Ralph, even
as a young child, loved to entertain his
brothers and sister, mother and father,
and others around him. He had 2 older
brothers, Albert (Al), Robert (Bob) and
an older sister, Muriel. Being closer in
age, Ralph and Muriel were especially

close in their relationship. Ralph had 2 younger brothers, Earl and LeRoy (Lee), Lee being the youngest.

(NOTE: For more information on my Dad's earlier life, refer to my Uncle Lee's Book, entitled Through The Years, by LeRoy Harlan Riesberg, an autobiography, October 1999.)

Like his brothers and sister, Ralph spent his childhood years going to school and doing chores on the farm in Sarona, Wisconsin. His mother ran the farm with the children's help while his father ran an Upholstery and Furniture Shop in Minneapolis during the week, coming to the farm on weekends.

In his spare time during his teen years, Ralph learned to play several musical instruments, including guitar, banjo, piano and drums. During his last 2 years in High School, while living with brother Bob and Bob's wife, Billie in Minneapolis, Ralph started his own Band and worked part time performing at dances and parties---which eventually led to him having his own Radio Show. With his "love for entertaining" and his exceptional musical talent, Ralph had formed his own orchestra, The El Patio Café Orchestra, performing on the Saturday Night Supper-Dance Club Radio Show which was broadcast from the El Patio Café (a popular place for dinner and dancing).

In the mean time, the movie star, Gloria Swanson and her school days best friend, Garnet, who both grew up in Minneapolis, would often come to the Supper-Dance Club. That is where they met Ralph and quickly became good friends with him. As a matter of fact, Ralph and Garnet became <u>such</u> good friends that they decided to get married---and did just that! But the marriage to Garnet did not last but about a year (according to my Mom, all Garnet would do all day is spend the day "beautifying herself"---no housework, no cooking, no nothing).

Then came the Stock Market Crash of 1929 and the ensuing Great Depression. Many, many, many jobs were lost including Ralph's (he had to disband his Orchestra). Fortunately, before long, he was able to get a traveling job selling Radio Commercials for the Radio Station for which he had previously worked. That is how he met my Mom,

Mae Moore, who was living with her brother, George in Shreveport, Louisiana and working as an Elevator Girl at the Captain Shreve Hotel. Ralph was staying at that Hotel working selling Commercials to the Radio Stations there in the Shreveport area. Ralph must have ridden the elevator at the hotel a lot because he and Mae started dating and before you knew it, they fell in love and got married. At that time Mae was 17 years old and Ralph was 23. After getting married, they moved to Tulsa, Oklahoma to be near my Grandmother, Nan in Pawhuska, Oklahoma. My Dad quit his traveling job selling Radio Commercials and went to work at Sears, Roebuck & Company selling appliances there in Tulsa.

Ralph had always liked music, going to Supper-Clubs and dancing (and it didn't take Mae long to start liking going there). They both loved dancing. Ralph also liked to drink and smoke. Mae didn't at first but as time passed, she eventually started smoking. Liking to dance, Ralph started dancing more and more with other beautiful young ladies, both married and single. As more and more good-looking men asked Mae to dance, Ralph would then get jealous, stop dancing, and go over to Mae and grab her by the arm and say, "let's go outside---I need to talk to you!" Once outdoors, Ralph was quite angry and would slap Mae in the face (this was my Mom's side of the story). I will never know the REAL truth until we all get to Heaven---but then, it won't matter anymore.

Ralph and Mae must have loved one another because they "hung in there" and stayed married for 9 years. I don't know if family finances were much of an issue back then in the mid-1930s, but Mae enrolled in and completed Beauty school to become Licensed as a Beautician. Then she opened her own Beauty Shop in their home. That was a very challenging accomplishment because Mae dropped out of school after the sixth grade of Elementary school. Mae had a very successful business for several years before I came into this world---and for 2 years afterwards. Five years after Ralph and Mae got married, I was born. My Mom worked very hard taking care of me in the home and running the Beauty Shop, as well. For 2 summers, my Mom's half-sister, Billie

Lee would come to Tulsa and spend most of the summer helping take care of me.

Then came the bombing of Pearl Harbor on December 7, 1941 by the Japanese, which started World War II. Like most men, my Dad enlisted in the Armed Services, in the U.S. Army. After completing Basic Training, my Dad was accepted into Officers Candidate School (OCS) at Fort Benning, Georgia. He was within 2 weeks of graduating from OCS when it was discovered that he had a Rheumatic heart condition from having Rheumatic fever as a child. Consequently, Dad was released from the Army with a Medical Discharge. He came back home to Tulsa to be with Mom and me. (Mom and Dad had been having some marital problems when Dad left to join the Army when W.W. II broke out.)

Anyway, Mom and Dad decided to start anew, for the 3 of us to move to San Diego, California; they sold their home and beauty shop and Dad transferred to Sears Roebuck there. We lived in San Diego for 6 months but Mom and Dad were still not getting along very well. The next thing I remember is the three of us being in a motel room somewhere between San Diego and Pawhuska, Oklahoma, with my Dad looking down at me and asking, "Do you want to stay with me or to go see Nan?" I picked my Grandmother, Nan (since I hadn't seen her in about a year)---the rest is <u>history</u>.

Less than a year after Dad and Mom divorced, my Dad got a Civil Service job working in Heating and Air Conditioning in the Ship Yards at Pearl Harbor in Honolulu, Hawaii. He worked there until the war was over in 1945. After the war, he transferred into the Facilities Maintenance Department at Camp Smith, a naval facility near Pearl Harbor.

After having enjoyed several years of bachelorhood living in Hawaii, Dad met an exotic, island woman who was working selling tickets at the Waikikian movie theater. Her name was Julia (Julie) Arnold, a widowed mother of 2 teenage children, a girl and a boy. Dad liked going to the movies a lot! It wasn't long before he and Julie started dating and going to the movies <u>together</u> (Dad didn't have to pay admission for her--- she got in FREE). They must have seen lots of <u>serious</u> movies because they started getting <u>serious</u>. In 1948, they got married. This was my Dad's third marriage---as they say, "the third time is the <u>charm</u>!" They were married in Honolulu but honeymooned in the United States---with their 3 children: Julie's: Betty Lou, age 17 and David, age 15; Ralph's: Rollie, age 10 (me). We made a 5 week driving trip <u>together</u> from Oklahoma up through the mid-west to Minnesota and Wisconsin to visit relatives and on to the north-east (New York); then back to Oklahoma to drop me off. (You can imagine all the fun with "skinny, all knees and elbows" me "crammed down" in the back seat of the car between 2 "big" teenagers.) Anyway, whatever I had to do, I <u>loved</u> being with my Dad, under any circumstances.

Many years later, after Loretta and I got married and had our Son, Doug, we got to see Dad a lot more often than I had been able to during my childhood years. Every couple of years, Dad and Julie would fly to Atlanta to visit us and we would fly to Honolulu (Kaneohe) to visit them. It wasn't always easy entertaining and making Julie happy because I don't think she really wanted to come visit us anyway. I was just <u>thankful</u> to see my Dad whenever and however I could!

I thank God for giving me my Dad. He and my Mom, when I was born, could have given me up for adoption--- but they didn't. I am proud of my Dad and have loved him more than <u>anything</u>! Before I met Jesus and let Him come into my heart, my Dad was my God. My Dad did the best he could, but I believe that he really did not want the responsibility of being a husband and a father.

-Best Job: Leader of his own Orchestra; Maintenance Supervisor, Public Works Dept.-- Honolulu, HI (tie)
-Worst Job: Working on his Mom & Dad's farm doing chores during childhood years.

(10) Mayme (Mae) Mary Moore
Riesberg Crow
-Born September 18, 1916
Orange, Texas
-Deceased: 1974 New Orleans,
Louisiana
-Parents: James Moore and
Nettie (Nan) Marie Landry
-Nationality: Irish, French

-Personality: Mae was a caring,
outgoing and spirited, intelligent, hard-
working, creative person. She had a
brother, George, who was 2 years
younger than her. She loved her little
brother very much and had to help her
Mother take care of him because their
Father died of a sudden heart attack

when she was 4 and her brother was 2. Immediately, their Mother, Nan went to work cooking and keeping house for other families while Mae watched George and did light chores. There was plenty of delicious food which the families gave them as "left-overs" but not enough money for paying all of the bills. Then, as I wrote in Chapter 3, Nan got a big break and was hired by the Governor of Oklahoma to be the "live-in" cook and nanny for he and his family. However, there was one catch---Mae and George could not live with their Mother in the Governor's Mansion. (They had to go live in the Catholic Orphanage.)

During the 3 plus years Nan was the cook and nanny for the Governor, she became acquainted with a nice looking, young man (he came from Greece as a teenager) who was working his own farm near Oklahoma City, growing and selling vegetables and fruits. One of his largest accounts was the Governor's Mansion. His name was Mike Poulos. As he came to the Mansion several times each week to deliver his "fresh off-the-farm" produce, he and Nan got to be very good friends. Eventually, they started dating on Nan's one night a week off. Before long, the relationship started turning serious and they decided to get married.

Once Nan and Mike married, Mike wanted Nan to quit her cook/nanny job and move with him to Pawhuska, Oklahoma where he had a much larger farm with a small house on the edge of town, along side Bird creek. Of course, the Governor and his wife begged Nan not to quit her job and leave, but told them that this would be an opportunity for her to have her young children, Mae and George back living with her again. So, the 4 of them moved to Pawhuska to start a new life together.

A couple of years after settling down to their new life, Mike and Nan started expanding their family. The first little baby girl born was named, Billie Lee; two years later, Katherine Lee (Katy) was born.

Things went well for the first few years---then family problems between Mike and his 2 step-children, Mae and George began to arise. The next thing that happened was Mae and George found themselves being placed in Catholic Church Orphanage there in

Pawhuska. (It was an "in-again", "out-again" situation for them for the next 5 to 6 years.) Finally, George quit school after the sixth grade and ran away from home to go live with one of his Mother's sisters, Aunt Hattie in Shreveport, Louisiana (Mae followed suit 2 years later). <u>NOTE</u>: Mom told me many times that some of the Nuns in the Catholic Home were mean to her and her brother (she never qualified "how" they were <u>mean------she didn't like to talk about it)</u>.

Ten years had passed since Mae ran away from home in Pawhuska, OK to go live with her brother, George in Shreveport, LA. Mae and Ralph were divorced. Mae and her little boy, Rollie, had moved away from living with her mother, Nan and step-father, Mike and 2 half-sisters, Billie Lee and Katherine. Mae and Rollie were living in a one-bedroom, very small rental house across the alley from Union Elementary school. Mae did not have a job but was dating a young, nice-looking divorced man, James (Buck) Crow, who was stationed in the U.S. Army at Fort Sill, OK. It was 1943 and W.W. II was going on; some time late that year or early in 1944, Mae and Buck were married. In January of 1945, James (Jimmy) Brian Crow was born.

In August of 1945, World War II finally ended (with the surrender of the Japanese). Buck was Honorably Discharged from the Army and came back home to Pawhuska to start a new civilian life with his family. He started his own Carpentry business and bought a nice, little, one-bedroom, one bathroom house with a screened-in back porch (which became the second bedroom with 2 beds).

In January 1948, William (Winky) Alfred Crow was born. Later that year, while at work, the ladder on which Buck was standing, fell with his right arm being between the ladder and the ground (his right arm was "crushed" at the elbow). The arm eventually healed but healed stiff, with very limited movement capability. From that point on, family life began a rapid deterioration. Mae and Buck ultimately went through a number of divorces and re-marryings---until they eventually stopped going through the formalities. NOTE: As my brothers, Jimmy, Winky and I have often times said to one another, "Mom and Pop

(Buck) could <u>not</u> live with one another---and could <u>not</u> live with<u>out</u> one another---they simply <u>jived</u> one another!"

In the later years after my brothers and I grew up, got married and had families of our own, Mom's mental condition worsened---no wonder with all of the "ups and downs" of her life. True, she "dwelled" on herself and her own life too much (I used to tell her when I was in High School and still living at home, "Mom, you need to <u>quit</u> dwelling on yourself and <u>start</u> thinking about and caring for others). I believe she was listening to what I told her after all, because her later years were spent with her being a Nurse's Aide, caring for other people (patients) at Saint John's Hospital in Tulsa, OK. She became very emotionally attached to many of the patients she helped care for---one particular patient who also became a good friend was Kenneth Weinburg, Sr., who was dying of Cancer. (After Mr. Weinburg's death, Mom married his son, Kenneth, Jr. (Ken), who had come often to the hospital to visit his dad before he died.) Ken took very good care of our Mom during those last 2 years before she died of Cancer (my

Brothers and I will always be grateful to Ken for the loving care he gave her)! NOTE: Mom dedicated her body to Cancer Research.

I thank God for giving me my Mom. She stuck with me through "thick and thin", good times and bad. She gave me the encouragement to succeed in life --- to always strive to do my best. She taught me the importance of being close to God and attending Church. I have loved her so very much!

-Best Job: Her own Beauty Shop (The Modern Wave); NOTE: Her "Dream" was to be a famous writer of stories: When I was a teenager, she was always staying up late at night writing stories on note book paper with a ball point pen; when finished, she would mail the stories to Woman's Day and Family Circle magazines---her stories were never accepted or published.

-Worst Job: Probably doing chores in the Catholic Church Orphanage/Home; and working on the farm as a child.

(11) <u>James (Jimmy) Brian Crow</u>
     -Born January 22, 1945
     Pawhuska, Oklahoma
     -Parents: James (Buck) Sylvester
     Crow and Mayme (Mae) Mary
     Moore Riesberg Crow
     -Nationality: Irish, French, other

-Personality: Jimmy is a caring, outgoing, intelligent, hard-working, determined, active person. Jimmy had a half-brother, Rollie who was almost 7 years old when he was born. Three years later, his "little brother" Bill (Winky) was born. As a young child, Jimmy loved attention and being in the middle of whatever was going on. His "big brother"Rollie, who loved him very much, gave him lots of attention---except one time. That time, being when Jimmy had just started walking at the age of about one year. Their Mom, who was talking with a lady friend in the school yard with a 15 feet high slide, told brother Rollie to watch his little brother to make sure he didn't get hurt. Well, Rollie was playing with the lady's little boy who was about Rollie's age. From time to time Rollie would look at Jimmy to make sure he was safe and okay. After a few moments had passed, Rollie looked around for Jimmy and he was not to be seen. Rollie immediately looked over at the slide (there Jimmy was, climbing up the steps, about three-fourths of the way to the top). Before Rollie could take 2 steps, running to the slide, Jimmy lost his hold and fell all the way to the ground, landing on his head! It scared all of us "to death", especially me since I was supposed to be watching him! Mom got to him before I could; when she picked him up off of the ground, Jimmy had a big bruise knot on his forehead and was screaming (I thought I had killed my little brother).

I thought Mom was going to kill me but she didn't. I did get a very severe scolding though. Mom and I rushed home (we lived just across the alley from the school yard) and Mom bandaged Jimmy's wound--- people very seldom went to the Doctor back in those days (most People didn't have Health Insurance or money to pay a doctor). Anyway, Jimmy's forehead eventually healed and he ended up growing up to become a nice looking, smart young man.

Jimmy's teen years were tumultuous with Mom and Pop's constant "battling" and on-again, off-again marriages. Mom ended up "farming out" Jimmy with Aunt Billie Lee, Uncle Damon and Katherine Lee while she and Winky went to Hawaii, unannounced, for Mom to try to get Rollie's Dad to come back to her (he had remarried in 1948 and this was 1958). Anyway, the stay in Hawaii lasted less than a week---Rollie's Dad said that she and Winky could not stay in Hawaii and had to go back to Tulsa. Once back in Tulsa, Mom did not bring Jimmy back home to live with her and Winky. Jimmy spent the rest of his teen years living with his aunt, uncle and cousin---he quickly became their "house servant". As soon as he graduated from High School (he couldn't wait), he moved out and got his own apartment. At the time, he was working full time as a Cashier/Stocker for Standard Humpty Dumpty, the same super market chain his brother Rollie had worked for during his high school days.

Finances weren't working out very well and he broke up with his girlfriend, so Jimmy decided to join the U.S. Army---at least there would be <u>free</u> room and board and the pay would be a little better. In the Army he was assigned to the Medical Corps as a Laboratory Technician. He enjoyed the work but the pay was considerably lower than what he could make as a civilian---so he took his Honorable Discharge after 4 years of service.

As a civilian once again, Jimmy got a good job as a Lab Technician and enrolled in college at Oklahoma University at Norman, OK. Thinking that he wanted to be a High School or College coach, Jimmy graduated with a degree in Physical Education. Realizing that he <u>really</u> liked the laboratory work more, he decided to go back to college, ending up with another degree, a B.S. in Physical Science. Many people really don't find out what kind of work they want to do until they reach middle-age or are near retirement. Jimmy was fortunate to realize early in life that he enjoyed working in the Medical field.

While working as the Laboratory Manager for a Doctors Group in Tulsa, OK, Jimmy met, dated and eventually married Martha. After a few years, James Brian, Jr. was born. A number of years later, when Brian Jr. was about 10 years old, Jimmy and Martha came to the realization that the marriage wasn't working out---so they parted ways and divorced.

To make a change of scenery, Jimmy decided to move to Baton Rouge, Louisiana to be close to his younger brother, Winky (now Bill). While living there, working for a Doctors Group laboratory, he met Chris, who was a Staff Attorney for the State of Louisiana. There was an immediate strong attraction between the two of them---they dated for a little while, fell in love quick and got married. (And they are still very happily married today!) A couple of years after marrying Chris, Jimmy (now Brian) was able to get (with his strong medical background) a position as Head of the Medicaid Department (Administrator) for the State of Louisiana. He held that position for almost 15 years before retiring May 1, 2008 to a life of golf and leisurely living (he and Chris' new home is located near the 11th hole of the community golf course). He is now <u>finally</u> "reaping the harvest" for all of his many years of hard work and sacrifice!

I thank God for giving me my "little brother" Jimmy. Having him and my other "little brother" Winky, taught me, as a young boy, how to deeply love and care for someone else other than myself. I cherish those years of caring for my brothers, especially at Christmas-time and on their birthdays. (I have loved thcm both so very much!)

-Best Job: The Administrator of the Medicaid Department for Louisiana.
-Worst Job: Chief-cook, bottle-washer and house keeper for Aunt Billie Lee and Uncle Damon.
(12) <u>William (Winky) Alfred Crow</u>
-Born January 16, 1948 Pawhuska, Oklahoma
-Deceased: September 1, 2006 Baton Rouge, Louisiana

-Parents: James (Buck) Sylvester Crow and Mayme (Mae) Mary Moore Riesberg Crow
-Nationality: Irish, French, other

-Personality: Winky was a caring, outgoing, intelligent, hard-working, determined, active person. He was very kind to others, often to the point of being self-sacrificing. (He and Jimmy had so many friends---at Winky's funeral service, the chapel was literally filled, while many others were waiting outside but could not get in until after the service was concluded).

As a young child, Winky had a very vivid imagination---he loved to make up and tell stories. Sometimes, he would even add his "own twist" to something that had actually happened, changing it to make it more exciting and colorful. Being the "baby brother", he got a lot of attention from big brothers, Rollie and Jimmy.

When Winky was a baby, their Mom put him in footed sleeper pajamas to sleep in at night---it got quite cold at night in Oklahoma during the winter. One day, brother Rollie told Mom, "baby Bill is so cute, he looks like Wee-Willie-Winky, the Fisk Tire Baby". (From that time on, baby Bill became known as Winky.)

Winky's teen years, like Jimmy's, were also tumultuous and riddled with very "hard times". This writing could not do justice to just how bad those years were for them.

When Winky was 15, Rollie brought him back to Shreveport to live with him because their Mom had been hospitalized for treatment for severe mental problems. Winky enrolled in the 9th grade at the high school nearby, made the football team and got a part time job as a car-hop at the local A & W Root Beer Stand. Things were going well for several months; brother Rollie was working the ramp for Delta Air Lines full time and was attending college at Centenary College taking 10-12 hours per semester. Winky was making good grades and doing well in football. But then---Rollie found out that Winky had been "skipping" school, and consequently, his grades were slipping fast. Of course, Rollie got <u>very</u> upset with Winky, giving him probably the worst "tongue lashing" he had ever had in his entire life. (To Rollie, getting a very good education was the <u>most important thing</u> in life---the <u>ONLY WAY</u> out of poverty and hunger!) Anyway, when Rollie got home from work late that night, Winky had left Rollie a "good-bye note", saying that he was leaving to go back home to Tulsa---even though there was no physical home to go to. For a while, he lived with brother Jimmy in his apartment. He got his own car once he became 16---Winky often times slept in his car. (He was working nights and weekends at Standard Humpty Dumpty super market and going to high school during the day).

After graduating from high school, Winky got a full time job as a draftsman with an oil company in Tulsa and attended Tulsa University almost full time, majoring in Electrical Engineering. Within 3 years, Winky had been promoted to Electrical Engineer with the Oil Company but job constraints and travel requirements were such that he had to withdraw from college. He deeply regretted having to drop out of college, but on-the-job experience he acquired designing oil refinery and processing facilities electrical schematic plans proved invaluable to him in his later working years. He worked for many major oil companies through the years as a direct-employee and as a contract-employee, designing facilities electrical lay-outs/plans at many manufacturing sites domestically and overseas, especially in the Middle East.

Winky was married and divorced several times. But his last marriage was the charm---he and Rene met at an oil company they both worked for and were just good friends for several years. Eventually, that good friendship started blossoming into a big romance. They were married in 1986. Two years later, they were blessed with a lovely daughter, Amber. At least God allowed Winky to live to see Amber graduate from high school. He is gone from us now---he was found to have Cancer of the Peritonaeal wall of the stomach about a year before he died. Those last 2 months of utmost, intense suffering was unbearable for Winky. We know that Rene and Amber miss him so very much and are totally lost without him, as are the rest of the family. (Words cannot convey how terribly much Jimmy and I miss him!)

I thank God for giving me my "little brother", Winky. Having him and my other "little brother", Jimmy, taught me, as a young boy, how to deeply love and care for someone else other than yourself. I cherish those years of caring for my brothers; I have loved them so very much!

-Best Job: Facilities Electrical Design engineer for oil companies.
-Worst Job: In the Seafood restaurant business with Aunt Billie Lee.

(13) <u>Nettie (Nan) Marie Landry</u>
<u>Moore Poulos</u>
-Born May 4, 1898 Gonzales,
Louisiana
-Parents: Records not available
(parents immigrated from France)
-Nationality: French

-Personality: Nan was a very loving, intelligent, hard-working, determined, steadfast, dependable, creative person.

Nan had 2 older sisters, Hattie and Sophie and a younger brother, Maurice.

In order to avoid being redundant, this Family Personal Profile on Nan will be brief (I have shared much about my

Grandmother's life in my Mom's Profile and my own).

I thank God for giving me Nan. She was always there for me and my brothers, whatever our needs were---to provide us with a shoulder to cry on, someone to listen to our problems, to have someone to tell us she loves us and is proud of us, someone to offer us encouragement, someone to feed us delicious food when we were hungry and most important of all, to have the sweetest, most precious Grandmother in the whole, wide world to love back! Her love for us was <u>unconditional</u>. She worked so very hard to get money to buy my brothers and I Christmas and Birthday gifts: our first and only bicycle, Bulova wrist watch, leather jacket, Shaeffer pen and pencil set, to name some. This world hasn't been the same without her! My brothers and I have loved her so, very much!

-Best Job: Cook/Nanny for Gov. of OK.
-Worst Job: Working in the fields/garden.

(14) <u>George Monroe Moore</u>
        -Born May 5, 1918 Orange Texas
        -Deceased: 1976 Shreveport, Louisiana

-Parents: George Monroe Moore and
Nettie (Nan) Marie Landry Moore
-Nationality: Irish, French

-Personality: George was a caring,
straightforward, intelligent, ambitious,
hard-working determined, studious
person.
 George worked hard all of his life
striving to achieve ever-increasing
life's goals he set for himself. Having
quit school in the 6th grade, he ran
away from home to go live with an
aunt in Shreveport, Louisiana.
However, things did not work out with
that arrangement. George got a job as a
dishwasher at a local café. He had no

place to live so he slept under a bridge viaduct for several months. Then the café owner found out that George had no home, so he let him sleep in the back storage room. About a year later, he saved enough money to get a one-room apartment. A year after that, his sister, Mae ran away from home and came to live with him, with them sharing rent and living expenses. Mae got a job as an elevator operator at the Captain Shreve Hotel. In the mean-time, George got a much better paying job as a railroad yard helper with Kansas City Southern Railway. He eventually went to night school and got his High School Diploma. Afterwards, he was promoted to Switchman with the railroad. Mae had already met Ralph, gotten married and moved to Tulsa, OK.

By this time, George had moved into his own home and met Thelma. They started dating, fell in love and eventually got married. The marriage went well for a number of years. Then George discovered that Thelma was seeing someone else while he was at work---the marriage abruptly ended in divorce.

George had his sights set all along on eventually becoming a Locomotive Engineer. It took almost 10 years of hard work and rigorous, extensive studying and testing but he finally achieved his ultimate goal---in 1958, he was promoted to Engineer with Kansas City Southern Railroad.

The year 1958 was very good to George. That year he met the divorced daughter, Billye Bryant, of a fellow, more senior engineer with the railroad. George and Billye started a relationship that quickly turned romantic (by the end of that year, they were married). Two years later, their precious daughter, Marie was born (she was George's one and only child; Billye had a son, Robert from her former marriage).

I thank God for giving me my Uncle George. Second to my Dad, I looked up to him and endeavored to pattern my life after him and his life. I was proud of him and have loved him so very much! When I was 12 years old, he came to Pawhuska to visit family and to "show off" his brand-new 1950 Ford (he taught me how to drive then, in his <u>new</u> car).

-Best Job: Railroad Locomotive Engineer.
-Worst Job: Café dishwasher; Working on step-father's (Mike) farm in the hot summer (tie).

(15) Michael (Mike) Poulos
-Born 1894 Southern Greece
-Deceased: Approx. 1982
Bartlesville, Oklahoma
-Parents: Records not available
(Parents remained in Greece)
-Nationality: Greek

-Personality: Mike (known as Gramps to the grandchildren) was a caring, intelligent, hard-working, adventuresome person.

Mike came to America from Greece with 2 friends who were brothers, Tom and Bill Javalous; Mike was 15, Tom 15 and Bill 13. Their families made their living by farming in the southern part of Greece. Mike, Tom and Bill saved the money they made working on the farms for a number of years to get enough money to pay for the ocean voyage to New York City. To save as much money on the fare as they could, they got passage on a freighter ocean-going vessel that could accommodate a small number of paying passengers. Friends back in Greece had told them about land being cheap to buy and farming conditions being good in Central and Eastern Oklahoma; once they docked In New York, they headed for Oklahoma. (Most of their money had been spent on the fare for the ocean-crossing, so they traveled to Oklahoma, part by "hitch-hiking" and part by bus.)

Many years later after marrying Nan, settling down in Pawhuska, OK and having and raising his family, in addition to farming, he was elected Con-stable for Osage County and Pawhuska---a position he held for many years.

I thank God for giving me my Grandfather, Gramps. He was always good to me and was proud of me. I have loved him very much! When I was a baby, when Mom and Dad would bring me to visit my grand-parents, Gramps would take me for a ride in his GMC pickup truck. (One time when he was taking me for a ride, the right front wheel came off of the truck, bringing the truck to an abrupt stop---I was suddenly thrown to the floorboard.) Fortunately, I was not hurt---just scared. As I got older, every time I would go visit Nan and Gramps, he would always tell me about that time when I was a baby and he thought he had killed me when the wheel came off of the truck.

-Best Job: As Constable, was personal
Chauffeur and travel escort
for the Honorable Judge Leahe of
Osage County.
-Worst Job: unknown

    (16) <u>James (Buck) Sylvester Crow</u>
        -Born 1913 Pawhuska, Oklahoma
        -Deceased: Approx. June 16, 1973
         Pawhuska, Oklahoma
        -Parents: Alfred Crow and mother
         (name not remembered)
        -Nationality: Irish, other

-Personality: Buck was a caring,
outgoing, athletic, hard-working,
intelligent person.
    He had an older sister, Daisy and an
older brother, Dick. His father, Alfred
was a U.S. Marshall. (Alfred taught

his sons how to hunt and helped them to become excellent marksmen.) Being very athletic, Buck was Captain of the football and basketball teams at Pawhuska High School (many of the School athletic records set by him have not been broken). He had a full Scholarship for football at Oklahoma University but he dropped out of college after the first semester---the regimentation of college was not for him.

When World War II broke out, Buck enlisted in the U.S. Army. He took his Basic Training at Fort Sill, Oklahoma. He was such an excellent marksman, the Army sent him to Gunnery School there at Fort Sill. (After completing that school, he was selected to become a Gunnery Instructor which required that he remain there at Fort Sill rather than having to ship over-Seas to go into combat.) He remained there until the end of WW II.

Sometime in 1943, while home on leave in Pawhuska, he got reacquainted with Mae and they started dating (they just barely knew one another in school since he was 3 years older than her). They got married in 1944. In

1945 Jimmy was born. In 1948 Winky was born. Now Rollie had 2 little brothers whom he loved very much.

From 1946-48, the family was doing well; they had a home of their own and Buck had a good-paying job with his own Carpentry business. Then, one day on the job, Buck had an accident and fell off of a ladder and crushed his right elbow---the arm healed stiff and would not bend. From that time on, he mostly tried to make a living by gambling (playing Poker, Dominoes and Billiards)--- with limited success.

The worst part was that he, many times, would be gone 2, 3, 4 weeks at a time without us knowing where he was. When there was no longer any food in the house, Rollie would ride his bicycle to the various places in town where Buck (Pop as he was called by his sons) usually gambled. Sometimes Rollie could find him, sometimes he couldn't. When Rollie did find him---and he was "winning", he would give Rollie $2-3 to go buy food with; if he was losing, he would say, "sorry, son, I don't have any money." (This is one of the main reasons Rollie has been working since he was 7 years old---to have money to buy food for he and his brothers when they got hungry.)

I loved Pop, my step-father very much. He was always good to me (as good or better than to his own sons). However, I do hold some resentment for the way he treated our Mom, especially in those middle to later years---and for those long periods of absence from home and the family. We have felt that he really did not want the responsibility of being a husband and a father.

-Best Job: Owning his own Domino & Poker Parlor in Tulsa, OK in his later years.
-Worst Job: Milk delivery route.

(17) &

(18) <u>LeRoy (Lee) Harlan Riesberg</u>
  -Born April 4, 1919 Minneapolis,
   Minnesota
  -Parents: August Sigfried Riesberg
   and Helga Theresa Moss
  -Nationality: Swedish, Norwegian

Figure 45
Lee, Earl, Muriel, Ralph, Bob and Al (1955)

  -Personality: Lee is a caring, outgoing
   ambitious, intelligent, hard-working,
   creative person.
  (<u>NOTE</u>: For more information on my
  Uncle Lee's and Aunt Kay's earlier
  lives, refer to his Book entitled,
  <u>Through The Years</u> by LeRoy Harlan
  Riesberg, autobiography, October
  1999.)
    In the spring of 1938, Lee met "that
  certain someone", Agnes Kay Pulaski

(Aggie, as friends and family called her). When the "love bug bites" who can resist! Lee and Aggie (Lee prefered "Kay") got married on September 1, 1939. Through the years, they had four children, Renee, Jim, Jon and Larry. Most of those years, the family lived in Denver, Colorado.

Agnes (Kay) Polaski Riesberg
-Born June 16, 1921 Minneapolis, Minnesota
-Deceased: August 8, 1988 Denver, Colorado
-Parents: Tony and Bertha Polaski
-Nationality: Polish, other

-Personality: Kay was a caring, outgoing, steadfast, dedicated, intelligent, hard-working person.

I have loved my Uncle Lee and Aunt Kay very much. They have always been there for me when I needed them. They were there in Hawaii, with loving care for me, when my Dad died July 28, 1978 (my whole world came "crashing down" on that day---I didn't want to live any longer). I will always appreciate them helping me get through that most difficult period of my life! I thank God for them!

-Best Job (Lee): Thirty-seven years with the General Services Administration, Real Estate Division.
-Worst Job: One year during the Great Depression as a Stock-person with Sears Roebuck & Company.

-Best Job (Kay): Homemaker, Wife & Mother.
-Worst Job: unknown.

(19) <u>Douglas (Doug) Edward Robertson</u>

-Born December 18, 1912 Tyronza, Arkansas

-Deceased: February 15, 2002 Memphis, Tennessee

-Parents: Christopher Columbus Robertson and Carrie Lula Gammill Robertson

-Nationality: Scotch, Cherokee Indian, English

-Personality: Douglas was a caring, somewhat outgoing, intelligent, extremely hard-working, ambitious, innovative, creative, talented person.

In a family of 3 siblings, Douglas was the only boy. He had an older sister, Berlean and a much younger (18 years) baby sister, Laverne. When he was a Senior in high school, his mother gave him the job of washing his baby sister's diapers in a wash-tub over an open wood-fire in the back yard (which resulted in heavy teasing from his friends and school classmates).

Douglas grew up not knowing anything but hard work. His many chores and jobs beginning as a young boy consisted of :

- Working on his parent's farm and doing his chores
- Cutting and selling fire wood
- Once the family moved to Memphis, Douglas had a newspaper route.
- During Junior High and High School, had a part time job working as an office boy; also started a wholesale egg business which he turned over to his father since his father had lost his job. (His father eventually bankrupted the egg business.)
- Worked as a Food Merchandise Broker, calling

on super markets for General
Foods Company

- Worked various jobs at
Firestone Tire & Rubber
Company with increasing
supervisory responsibilities
from Tire Builder, Inspector
and ultimately, Quality
Control Department Problem
Specialist supervisor.

After Douglas graduated from
high school, he married his high
school sweetheart, Marietta Jones.
After 5 years of working hard and
saving their money for vacation, he
and Marietta went on vacation
trips to places like Mexico, Canada
and the United States southwest and
northeast; then Loretta Claire was
born. Five years later, Loretta's
baby brother, Douglas Edward, Jr.
(Eddie) was born.

I thank God for bringing Douglas,
my father-in-law into my life! I
have loved him very much! In some
ways, he has been better to me than
my own Dad. (After Loretta and I
married, he was always there for me
when I needed him.) He taught me a
lot about building things and how to

constructively question how and why mechanical things work.

He also was a victim of a controlling, abusive family member (his mother). Of course, it was a generational sequence of genetics at work (his mother's mother had the same personality traits and abusive actions). Perhaps that had a lot to do with his marital relationship with his wife, Marietta. In the earlier years of their marriage, they had a half-way normal relationship. However, Douglas maintained a strong, controlling position in the marriage and family---it was as though Douglas was continuously, <u>silently</u> saying, "no woman will ever control my life and tell me what to do again!" (Douglas did the best he could, but I believe that he really did not want the responsibility of being a husband and a father).

On the positive side, Douglas was innovative and very creative. His hobbies (which should have been his jobs and own businesses) consisted of:

- Building his own two-story, large wood-working shop
- Going to antique shops and museums, drawing sketches, taking dimensions and going home to his shop and making that item (which looked as good or better than the original he copied)
- Copying weaving looms, modifying them to make the design more effective and efficient, and then, teaching himself to weave and make copies of Navajo Indian tapestries and rugs; also to design and weave his own creations (which were "treasures beyond belief").

Unfortunately, those beautifully creative skills of his died when he died---no one in the family took the time to spend with Douglas for him to teach these artistically, price-less skills to them.

-Best Job: Hobbies.
-Worst Job: Food Merchandise Broker/Salesman (for having to "push", sell supermarkets merchandise they didn't need).

(20) <u>Marietta Jones Robertson</u>
-Born October 9, 1916 Pocahontas,
Tennessee
-Parents: Robert Winston Jones and
Lela Tennys Gurley
-Nationality: Welsh, Irish

-Personality: Marietta has always
been an affectionate, dedicated, self-
sacrificing, talented, intelligent,
outgoing, hard-working person.

Marietta grew up seeing an almost perfect marriage between her mother and father (Lela and Robert). She never once heard them argue. But that wonderful marriage ended suddenly and much too soon--- Marietta's father was stricken with Cancer and died right after she had just graduated from high school. She and Douglas got married (Douglas was 4 years older and had already been out in the "cruel world" working at a regular job). Going into marriage, Marietta thought she was going to have a near-perfect marriage, just like her parents had. The first few years went pretty well. Five years into the marriage, a cute little, red-headed baby girl, Loretta was born; five years later, cute, little, baby boy, Eddie was born.

A few more years passed, and with Psychological wounds that were inflicted on Douglas by his mother (another "strong controlling personality") during his childhood years, Douglas started rebelling against the "institution of marriage", determined to break any hold that any woman might be getting on him (especially his wife).

One thing Douglas and Marietta had in common, they both loved to travel, especially to the western United States and Canada. (Every year for vacation, Douglas, Marietta, Loretta and Eddie would "pack up and head out".)

I thank God for bringing Marietta, my mother-in-law into my life! I have loved her very much! In some ways, she has been better to me than my own Mom. (After Loretta and I married, she has always been there for me whenever I needed her.)

-Best Job: Mother to her children; hobby was cook and seamstress.
-Worst Job: unknown.

(21) <u>Douglas Edward (Eddie) Robertson, Jr.</u>
   -Born March 20, 1946 Memphis, Tennessee
   -Deceased: July 19, 2005 Bowling Green, Kentucky
   -Parents: Douglas Edward Robertson, Sr. and Marietta Jones Robertson

-Nationality: Scotch, Cherokee Indian, Welsh, Irish

-Personality: Eddie was a caring, somewhat outgoing, intelligent, studious, ambitious, hard-working, innovative, person.

Being the baby of the family, Eddie got plenty of attention from his "big sister", Loretta (5 years older) who loved him very much. In his childhood years, his sister and his mother strived to protect him and take care of him because he seemed to be "accident-prone".

Being born not in the best of health, especially with a chronic sinus infection condition, Eddie's doctor prescribed that Eddie be taken to Florida for the summer. So, that summer of 1949, Marietta, Loretta and little Eddie (age 3) spent the summer in Clearwater, FL---Douglas (daddy) had to stay home in Memphis to earn a living for the family. Three months of exposure to the warm sun, tropical breezes and salty, cool ocean water helped Eddie's sinus condition a lot---and it brought out <u>all</u> of Loretta's freckles "out from hiding". But it was a big success (the kids had lots of fun in the sun).

Eddie's teen years were filled with music which he loved (the music of the '60s). During the high school and early college years, he was a drummer in several rock-n-roll bands---most notably was the "Escapades". A key member of this band, a guitarist and vocalist, was Garry Phillips (his father was Sam Phillips, Owner and Founder of Sun Records in Memphis, TN). They cut and released several single records but none were a big hit---the biggest being "Cadillac Man". (So much for timing and having "connections" in the show business world---.)

Mid-way through college, Eddie fell in love with and married his high school sweetheart, Sandra Berryhill. She worked full time and Eddie part time until he graduated 2 years later, with a Degree in Education/Journalism from Memphis State University. During the next several years, Meredith Claire was born and then, Ericka Leigh 3 years later.

The marriage between he and Sandra went well for several more years until Eddie got an out-of-town traveling job with a major publishing company, selling educational books. The rest is history---divorce and all.

Eddie (now Ed preferred) had numerous jobs but most of the later ones were in the Communications field (Ed eventually went back to college to get his Masters Degree in Communications). The job he held the longest was Director of Communications with Federal Express (he had over 25 years service when he retired). He still held the idea that he wanted to be a teacher (original degree was in

Education), so he accepted a contract with Western Kentucky University in Bowling Green, KY to teach Communications there.

Ed had met and married Cindy Lunn (another controlling personality), a divorced mother with 2 pre-teens children a few years before he retired from Fed Ex. He said he was happy but problems began to develop once Cindy's children reached adulthood, especially with her son.

I loved Ed (he will always be Eddie to us) very much! I loved him like my very own brother. I thank him most for giving me a Christmas gift in 1982---a book on Financial Planning written by a prominent female Financial Planner (this book, which she later autographed for me, changed my life and eventually led me to a career change to a profession of which I am now in, with my own Financial Advisory/Planning business).

-Best Job: Head of Corporate Communications with a major corporation.

-Worst Job: Bus-boy and dishwasher for a large restaurant (lasted one day---he was taking the tips left on the table by customers because he thought they were left for <u>him</u>).

(22) &

(23) <u>August Sigfried Riesberg and Helga Theresa Moss Riesberg</u>
(My Grandparents and my Dad's parents---I did not have the opportunity to know and be with them since my Dad and Mom divorced when I was 4 years old.)

Figure 9
August and Helga Riesberg with grandchildren (l-r) Gene Schreyer, Jeanne Riesberg, and Helga with Bobby Riesberg—1931

Figure 1
(r) August Riesberg, his friend Bert (they enlisted together) and unknown friend Company K, 15th Minnesota Volunteer, Camp McKenzie, Augusta, Georgia 1898

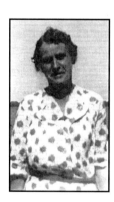

Figure 2
Helga Moss (1882) age 20

B. **<u>Thank You</u>**

- Our Lord and Savior, Jesus Christ for giving me the motivation, guidance and opportunity to write this book.
- My wife, Loretta for bringing me to Jesus.
- My former Sunday School Teacher and Assistant Pastor, Brother Jack May for bringing me to Jesus.
- Delta Air Lines for hiring Loretta Robertson as a Flight Attendant (Stewardess)---------without that, Loretta and I would have never met.
- Bill Phillips – owner of his own Insurance Agency for giving his employee, Loretta Robertson the afternoon off and suggesting "that she go to the airport to watch the airplanes take-off and land"---she didn't plan on doing so, but that is when she filled out an application to become a Stewardess for Delta Air Lines.
- Delta Air Lines for hiring me and giving me the opportunities they did.

- Our son, Doug and Daughter-in-law, Amy.
- Our family and friends who have given us support and encouragement.
- Memphis State University (now University of Memphis) and Centenary for giving me the opportunity to get a College Degree and a good, quality education.
- My college, high school and elementary school teachers for their dedication, hard work and support in helping me to learn and strive for higher goals of achievement.
- Our precious Grandsons for being who they are, for their love and for being here for us to have 4 wonderful guys to love and devote our lives to.

C. <u>Asking Forgiveness</u>

- I am asking for forgiveness from those whom I have wronged and sinned against.

- With Jesus' help and guidance, I have forgiven those who have hurt me and my loved ones.

D. **Book Dedication**

- I dedicate this book to my Lord and Savior, Jesus Christ who loves me in spite of my many flaws, sins and shortcomings.
- Although it is not my intent that monetary gains come from this book, but in case they do, I wish for those proceeds to be equally distributed as follows:
  1) The Billy Graham Crusade/Evangelistic Association -10%
  2) Love Worth Finding Ministries, Memphis, TN – 10%
  3) New Hope Baptist Church, Fayetteville, GA – 10%
  4) St. Jude Children's Research Hospital, Memphis, TN – 15%
  5) Our 4 precious Grandsons: Zachary, Jeremiah, Nathanicl and Ethan Riesberg – 10% (each)
  6) The Rolland G. & Loretta C. Riesberg Foundation, Inc. – 15%

E. Supplemental Information (Reference Material)

(1) ICSA (International Cultic Studies Association), Cultic Studies Review, Vol. 7, No. 1, 2008, pp. 57, <u>Adult Children of Parental Alienation Syndrone: Breaking the Ties that Bind</u>, by Amy J. L. Baker

(2) College for Financial Planning
8000 East Maplewood Ave.,
Suite 200
Greenwood Village, CO 80111
(866) 663-8911

(3) <u>Money Dynamics For The 1980s</u>, Venita VanCaspel, 1980, Reston Publishing Company, Inc.

(4) Society of Certified Senior Advisors™
1325 South Colorado Blvd.
Suite B-300-A
Denver, Colorado 80222-3305
(800) 653-1785
www.csa.us

The Patio Café Orchestra – Ralph Riesberg 1928

(Mom & Dad)
Mae & Ralph Riesberg
Wedding Photo (1933)

Loretta and Rollie

when

they

first

met!

NOTES:

• *Things I can do to improve <u>my</u> life:*

NOTES:

- *Things I can do to improve <u>my</u> life:*

_____

_____

_____

_____

_____

_____

_____

_____

_____

_____

_____

_____

_____

_____

_____

_____

_____

_____

_____